D1784484

A Meditative Parent

The Making of a triplet dad

S.C Wood

A meditative parent

ISBN:9781076579478

A meditative parent

This book is inspired by my daughters

Frankie Ava Blakely & Lacey

Never step too far away from kindness courage & the light you were born with

*

And to my wife Stacey

-One day we may get some peace and quiet

A meditative parent

CONTENTS

A meditative parent

ACKNOWLEDGMENTS

Thank you to Danny Schwarzhoff Snr for the meditation and your suggestions in getting me started with writing a book. Also, for the help you have given me on a personal level over the years. To Sarah Lawton Coombes (mumzilla.co.uk) for your time spent editing and your encouragement to get the best out of me as a first-time writer. A big thanks to Michael McGhee for your input and suggestions, that without my landing in the Orkney islands all those years ago I would not have had. And to my nephew Fin for your pc skills.

Thank you to all the family that have rallied by us throughout this life changing event, without whom it would have been so much more difficult. To my Mum for always believing in me through the worst of times and the best, and for all the help you give us. And to Di, there are not enough words to express my gratitude for the time and support you gave us when the girls were born and for the support you still give.

To Paddy (The Godfather). My most trusted confidant, and my good friend Donna, thank you for both being there on the end of the line through it all. For your help in keeping my feet on the ground in the times I unraveled, and for always pointing me back to faith and consciousness. A massive thankyou to all the NHS staff at St Michaels Bristol, Musgrove park Hospital Taunton and Yeovil district hospital who took such good care of us throughout the pregnancy through to the arrival of our girls.

To my daughters for inspiring me to strive for better. And to my wife. For the immense job you did of carrying our daughters and bringing them safely into this world, for being such a wonderful mother. For your understanding and support in the writing of this book. There is so much I owe you for this life we've made together. You're the strongest woman I know, and a testament to what motherhood is all about.

Preface

This isn't a parenting manual and I am not an expert. I come from a broken home and lived a damaged life before becoming a parent. It's not my place to tell anyone what to do, or the best way they should do it. I am now just a normal working guy who happens to have a background of serious mental health problems and alcoholism. I found recovery and emotional sobriety through a Non-contemplative meditation. A free exercise that contributed to the survival of myself and my family through the most stressful of events, simply by granting me the grace to consciously face the pressures of doubling my family unit in one hit.

In the February of 2018 I decided to make a start on this book. Partly because I was told by other parent's I would forget the early experience of having babies (a comment usually delivered with a sense of relief). But my main reason was that in discovering I was to be a father to triplets I found very few resources to give me a head's up as to what I may be facing. Especially as a first-time dad doing the baby deal.

This isn't a 'Whoopy-doo-dah, look at me I have got triplets' kind of book. And as much as it still amazes me, it has been one of the toughest events my family would go through - and are now happily still in the thick of.

I wrote this because the pressures we faced with a high-risk pregnancy had seemed unsurmountable, and the emotional strain of three babies on my marriage almost separated us. I want other parents to know that there is hope, that through sharing my story I can at least pass on something of value to anyone facing parenthood for the first time.

This is a book about dealing with the most important job anyone could have, at the time it matters the most. In becoming a loving parent from a past of self-driven destruction.

Introduction

A meditative parent

In the stream of life stress is inevitable, for a parent It is inescapable. As are the negative emotions that arise when we encounter difficult events that cause reaction. It may be a loved one being diagnosed with a serious illness – or arriving at the soft play centre with hungry screaming babies in the back of the car only to find it is closed. They both have the exact same ability to disrupt something inside of us. In this sense it is not just the tigers that will get us - it's the bunnies we really need to watch out for. It is the small events that we meet daily that chip away at our psyche and cause us to resent the world around us and judge others for their imperfections and mistakes. Yet we brush them off without a conscious thought, immediately suppressing the negativity we feel and carrying on with our day until we meet the next unexpected moment that causes us to emotionally react. It is much easier to justify our reactions to the bigger events in life than it is the smaller ones. But it becomes almost embarrassing to admit that the little things that piss us off can cause almost as much cumulative emotional trauma as those larger ones. We end up trapped in a cycle of resenting and suppressing negative emotions, struggling through life and getting relief wherever and whenever we can. Life is never going to be a breeze. But neither should it break us down from the inside out.

We grow ever more agitated and restless. If you already have children and are up against the daily stresses of a relentless demanding routine of work and homelife you may know this act well. You know what it is to be constantly tempted to react and resent your situation and feed the negative emotions that crop up from within throughout your day. The problem is that the negativity you suppress and do your best to ignore goes no-where. It attaches itself to you under the surface and creates all sorts of problems.

It's how symptoms like anxiety disorders and depression develop and there seems to be no tangible solutions to them. To seek relief becomes the only option. Yet those moments of distraction only refocus our attention away from the frustrations and guilt we experience for harbouring such negativity. We become victims of our own circumstances. The fixes we find to alleviate our internal discomfort serve only to bring temporary relief as life and our emotional states become harder to manage. And amongst this daily struggle we try to raise children. *But Imagine if you had a way to meet stress without becoming overwhelmed, and how different life would become for yourself and those directly around you as a result.*

It's no secret that most of us make our start in life in stressful environments. We are born into the hands of others who themselves are struggling to deal with the pressures of daily life. It is why we need to forgive our parents. They didn't know how to meet stress either. They suppressed it themselves and did the best they could. To resent them for their mistakes and impatience is a judgment we cannot afford to carry forward in life. That resentment will affect our own children in turn.

By chance, a few years ago I discovered a unique meditation. A metaphysical observation exercise that has drastically changed my path. Especially when it comes to dealing with fatherhood, the arrival of our triplets and the way I treat the people in my life who rely on my emotional consistency and patience. It has completely changed the way I meet the pressures of life. You will find the link to this free meditation in the back of this book.

I would not have survived the life event we faced together as a family had I not already found a way to stay awake to the rising negative emotions that came with it. If you are a parent who is struggling, I hope you find something within these pages to be of use. It is why I felt writing this book was such an important undertaking. It is a sad fact that many couples are not making it after the arrival of babies. Especially parents of multiples. The stress and pressures are too much to deal with. Yet I whole heartedly believe there is a solution that will contribute to a family staying the distance so that children can thrive in a loving environment free from the effects of stress. If the family unit has already broken apart there is even more reason to find consistency and emotional balance amongst the tense difficulties that can arise out of those situations. Children need stability in their lives from the two people who influence them the most.

Breakups of multiple parents seem to mainly happen within the first six months of the babies being born. It is why I have chosen to document the pregnancy and the first six months of the arrival of the triplets. And more importantly, document how I dealt with it from a mostly conscious perspective (I say mostly because as with all parents I had to face sleep deprivation when life becomes a case of buckle up and do your best). I know emotional consistency is possible no matter what your current situation. The solution lies in conscious awareness and the ability to observe our thoughts from a neutral position without being affected by them. To live in the meditative state, free from anger and fear. I will also share with you how I arrived at meditation and why It became such an intrinsic part of my daily life.

The Non-contemplative meditation I practice is simple and costs nothing. There are no hooks into religion. I don't have a guru, nor do I follow another person's directions. I am not a part of any meditation group or class. I don't have any rituals or Tibetan singing bowls. There is no chanting or patchouli incense burning with cool rain sound effects in the background to make my experience 'more trippy man'. I am not a Buddhist, nor am I part of any religious organisation. I don't buy any meditation cd's or bonus box sets that will further my minds expansion. I am not going to try and convince you that you need to meditate. That is your business and only you will know if you are ready. I can only share my personal experience.

I am a blue-collar welder. I love rock music (only the good stuff though) and my band. I have a family that come first, and I do my best to put their needs before my own. I meditate to remain conscious and awake in the stream of life and to improve as a husband, a father and a human being. And although I still make mistakes, and life continues to challenge me, I now meet the stresses of daily life with a certain courage, from a clear perspective of discernment rather than judgment. Which is a far cry from how I used to face life, full of resentment and fear.

Had I not discovered the meditation when I did, I don't believe that dealing with the pressures of a high-risk pregnancy and the subsequent stress around my family's circumstances would have been possible for me to cope with. Instead, at least for the most part I was able to stay awake to the rising negative emotions we faced each day.

Rather than getting overwhelmed by negative thinking and fears. Conscious awareness has now become the keystone of dealing with everyday life.

Chapter 1

Early days

I made my dramatic entrance into the world at the tail end of the sweltering summer of 1976. My stressed mum, whose waters had broken, and my dad were waiting in a side ward of a city hospital when my feet popped out, they were also blue. So, with no nurses around my dad scooped mum up off the bed and carried her shouting for help down the corridor of the ward until he was heard. I was a breech birth, born with the umbilical cord wrapped around my neck, navy-blue in colour and into stress and panic. With my brain deprived of oxygen my parents were told that they were facing a life of taking care of a little boy who would essentially be brain dead. I would never develop normally and would need 24-hour care. As it happened the doctors were wrong.

I was hard work as a kid, at the age of six a child psychologist was called to visit me in the hope of shedding some light on my inability to operate at less than a thousand miles an hour. At the end of the first and only assessment from her, the visitor reported to my mum that there didn't seem to be much wrong with me. At which point I came charging in from another room and dived off the sofa through an open window disappearing off into the field at the bottom of the garden screaming. ADHD was not really a thing back then. It was years later that my endless energy and complete lack of concentration was explained, and I would find a better understanding of my condition and a much calmer existence.

I lived obsessively in my head and was forever in a fantasy land. Most of the situations I day-dreamed about involved scenarios like me pulling people from a crashed burning car and becoming a hero for the world to see as I was paraded on TV on the evening news. Then everyone would finally see I was someone. I got high on those thoughts and was almost permanently lost in my thinking. I was going to show the world one day I was a hero – specifically, I was going to show my dad.

I was also a confused little boy, either over excited or frightened. From a very early age I was exhibiting sexualised forms of behaviour that must have been learned through the abusive behaviour of others, and which would have disturbed other people and caused me to believe I was born bad and different from others. As I grew older those memories plagued me as I came to realise more that they were not normal behaviours for a little boy. The problem was that I had no memory of any abuse, I was too young.

It was decades later when I finally spoke to someone about

11

that time of my life that I pieced together what had happened to me. But as a child growing up, knowing what I knew in my head made me feel isolated and scared. There was something horribly wrong with me and I knew it. I couldn't explain or talk to anyone about it. The memories became my horrible secret that I kept stuffed down, I was never going to let them come to light. No-one could ever know.

I concluded to myself by the age of around eight that I was born evil, and the reason my home life was so difficult was because my parents knew I was evil and couldn't bring themselves to discuss it with me. Each time there was a problem at home, no matter what the cause I felt I was to blame. I also believed it was the reason for the strained relationship with my dad. It was why he didn't seem to like me or have any time for me. And as for those early memories they never left me alone. The embarrassment, fear and shame I felt as a child remained with me. As did the voice that reminded me daily that I was no good and didn't deserve anything or anyone worthwhile in my life.

My self-harming behaviour started early as a result and came quite naturally to me. I liked to hurt myself and enjoyed the relief I found in the pain. I felt a sense of rightness within me about the act of cutting myself. It became another personal problem that would occasionally crop up on my journey whenever the pressures of life got too much. I also got quite inventive with it. I found many other ways to hurt myself as I grew older.

My father was a troubled man who struggled with prescribed morphine addiction, gambling and alcohol abuse. A result of harbouring anger around his own horrendous upbringing. He never wanted children. Neither myself nor my brother were planned, and my dad was at a loss with us while my Mum did her best with two unexpected boys on the Autistic spectrum.

My childhood was up and down as we moved to a new house constantly, relocating every one or two years, dragged in the wake of my father's ever deteriorating mental state. He had an obvious impatience and dislike towards me that I feared and resented him deeply for. All I ever wanted was his approval. For him to tell me I was going to be alright and that I was a good kid. He used to tell me I could either be his worst enemy or best friend. I just wanted a dad who was present and interested in me. Most of the time though I was his worst enemy. It wasn't that easy to be his best friend.

My days revolved around me as far back as I can remember. Deep down all I craved was some sort of normality in my life as I grew ever more restless and discontented at home. My school years were difficult. Had I stayed in one place it would have become apparent to my teachers that I had problems learning as I was permanently distracted, being forever pulled away by my imagination, too much to be able to concentrate and retain information. But with moving so much, at each new school I was instead seen as an awkward little shit who was trying my teachers on purpose. All my school reports read the same – "needs to concentrate more, is too easily distracted!" I used to dread taking them home for my dad to read.

During my years at home I grew ever more mentally detached from my family. It seemed to happen the more time I spent with friends. To see how other dads engaged with their sons just shone a brighter light on the difficulties I had with my own, and the shame and guilt around my earliest memories just detached me further from my family unit the older I got.

My dad worked hard as a poultry farmer. A house always came with his job and so we would up-sticks and disappear to a new county to resettle every time his feet got itchy enough. This routine of moving, being the new boy in the area along with my brother, having to make new friends, adapt to a different school with different teachers and new environments was an annual event I grew to hate. I got bullied with each move, by teachers as well as the kids who always liked to test the new kid on the block. I had learned very early in my life that when I was in fear, the best thing to do was to lie. So that's what I did, and I got good at it. I realised I could make things up about myself, usually about how tough I was and the string of schoolyard fight victories I carried on my belt. My protection mechanism of dishonesty never held up for long though. I wasn't very big as a kid and would always wind up getting my head flushed down the toilets by older kids sooner or later, or get my ass handed to me on a plate in the school yard or on the walk home. By the time I was finishing primary school, and because of all the bullying I was unable to go on to the local high school that was first choice for everyone in the area. Instead my brother and I went to a school twenty miles away where I didn't know anyone at all.

We used to catch the train early in the morning. The school seemed gigantic compared to the little village primary schools I was used to. I was a bit wiser by 11 and was less hasty to make myself out to be something I wasn't. I figured no-one knew me, so it was my chance to try and be myself. Problem was I was unsure how to do that, so I became the odd kid. I learned by imitating other kid's behaviours. Because of the fear under the surface I compensated by being completely over the top and acting the fool most of the time, I was either high up or low down, but I liked the school. I had to have special needs classes for my writing which got me a bit of stick from others at times, and occasionally I overstepped the marks with my unfiltered and off the wall sense of humour. But all in all, I did okay there. I made a few close friends and spent the beginning of my second year getting close to a girl I really liked. When she became my girlfriend, I felt happier than I had felt in a long time.

A month after we fell in love (not real love, but the sort of hormonal, over emotional teenage angsty relationship stuff that I thought was love when I was 13). I arrived home from school one day to the news my dad had taken a new job in a rural country village in a different county. We were going to visit the new house within the next few weeks and I would again be changing schools. My brother would be making the three-hour long commute by train and bus to the school to finish his exams.

There were lots of moments in my young life that I got overwhelmed by anger towards my dad. And the resentment I felt that day affected me deeply. I didn't know it at the time (I still believed the growing tension at home was caused by me), but we were moving because he had formed a bad gambling habit the year before when he got the news his dad had died. Home life had begun getting even more tense as his gambling addiction took off and his morphine intake and drinking stepped up a gear. Maybe he saw the opportunity to move as a fresh start in a new place. I just saw that I was being screwed over without being consulted. I had to say goodbye to the few friends I had made, and worst of all my first girlfriend. I still remember her face when I told her, she was hurt and refused to talk to me for my remaining time at the school. It tore me up.

It was the last time we would relocate as a family and my behaviours soon began changing. I started hanging around with other dysfunctional kids that I met in the village. I began stealing with them. I lied constantly to make myself out to be something I wasn't which quickly pushed friends at the new school away. My dishonest behaviour was all driven by fear and resentment. I also began to stop caring about myself and other people. At least I tried too, I had to learn not to get too attached because nothing to me was permanent. The rug could be pulled from under me at any-time, so it became my position to not let people get too close. And if I got too friendly with people I would walk away before I got hurt, or before I hurt them. I also discovered around that time that alcohol instantly numbed the internal pain, it was the beginning of a deadly relationship that would eventually all but destroy me.

That last move as a family, along with the emotional strain we were under with my dad's spiraling problems became too much to deal with for all of us. For my brother, my mum and myself. Everyone but me was medicated to mentally cope and there was little communication between any of us. We were all in our own way doing the best we could with the situation we were in.

Chapter 2

Leaving home

I sat quietly, my heart racing in my chest and the heat of fear rising to my face in my darkened moonlit bedroom. Hoping to hear silence fall in the house. I could hear the angry muffled roars of my drunken dad pacing around downstairs. In between the outburst I heard mum crying, probably trying to reason with him. And if we were lucky, he would tire out and stay down there if the whisky knocked him out fast enough. I was used to his outbursts. A couple of nights before I heard banging downstairs in the early hours of the morning, I crept down to see what was going on and saw him sat naked in the kitchen, crying and angry, hitting himself in the head with a saucepan to fix a headache. It was normal behaviour. It had been normal for years.

The shouting eventually stopped, the silence was followed by someone staggering up the stairs, it was obviously dad from the heavy slow steps. My door swung open and dad fell in and landed ass end on the edge of my bed, stinking of booze. "Son, you need to know something" he announced with a serious tone. "What's that dad?" I asked, as I curled myself up at the opposite end of the bed. "Drugs are really fucking bad for you, and I know you've been smoking pot, I

19

see how red your eyes are when you come back from your walks. You can't bullshit me!".

In truth the only drugs I knew of were the pills my older brother took for his depression and the "other good one's" he'd mentioned since leaving home the year before. Those and the morphine suppositories dad became addicted too and stuck up his ass every-day to help with his headaches. I honestly had no idea what he was talking about by suggesting I was getting high. I had no interest in drugs, I had watched what they had done to him and drugs frightened me. He had recently got a new device from the doctor that injected a shot of morphine straight into his leg. What I didn't know then was that his Doctor had already warned mum to "Get those boys out of that house". But she was as frightened of him as I was by that time. My brother had already gone, he made the decision to leave when he came home one evening from school to the shouts of "you fucking pig! you little cunt" and walked in on dad giving me a beating while my mum was trying to stop him. When my brother Rob told me he was leaving, he apologised for going and warned me that dad would probably take all his anger out on me now, but that he couldn't stay anymore. I resented him for going but understood his reasons. So, it was just mum, dad and me at home. And I lived on eggshells around him. Especially when he wandered into my room for a drunken chat.

Dad continued with his anti-drug rant, "I know all about drugs you know, I was young once too". I didn't doubt this late-night confession but felt it best to keep my mouth shut and let him get whatever he needed to say off his chest. "I used to smoke pot all the time, even your mum smoked it occasionally. We used to have the best acid back then, Black bombers, Ace of clubs". He went on, rejoicing in his personal hilarious stories of ripping off un-suspecting punters with oxo cubes wrapped in foil in the place of hashish. I was bored and wished he would just wrap it up and fuck off to bed. I was tired and had school the following morning, the last thing I needed was my drunk dad keeping me up by joyfully reminiscing on stories of how smashed he used to get back in the day.

After about an hour of painfully listening to him drivel on with what I could only make out to be a parental talk on the dangers of drugs, he finally got around to his reason for coming in that night." Son, can you get me some weed? I know your smoking it with your mates". This put me in a predicament. For one, I no idea how to get drugs, nor did I have any idea what I was buying if I could. But I also didn't want to disappoint my dad as it could really piss him off, already believing me, his youngest son was a pothead, I knew I would never convince him otherwise. "I'll see what I can do dad" I offered as I fought to keep my exhausted eyes open. "Good lad, I knew you could help your old dad". And off he went to bed.

I did what he asked and found him drugs, and in doing that for him I was offered, and took speed (amphetamine) as well as smoked marijuana. And once discovering the effect drugs had on me, I lost all fear of them.

I always did what dad asked of me, partly out of fear and partly out of desperately wanting his approval. But I had grown to resent and fear him. When I was 13, just after my brother left home and whilst dad was seeing a new psychiatrist, he took mum and me to the pub one lunch time to tell us all about how he'd been sexually abused as a child. How he had grown up in a house of abuse, incest and alcoholism. His dad, my Grandad was a sick man. Dad's psychiatrist had suggested he revisit all the places from his childhood the abuse took place to "Put the ghosts to rest" as he put it. He had planned a weekend away to do this trip and wanted to take me with him. I knew that this weekend away would involve drinking lots of alcohol, a past time which had already grown on me, and having no money knew he would be buying so I settled with that as an excuse in my mind to tag along. I also saw a chance to bond and be close. I thought if that happened, my fear of him would leave.

It was as I expected. We drove around rural Wales, drinking and occasionally stopping at sites of significance where he would tell me the horrible stories of what happened to him.

I learned a lot about the history of the dark childhood he had with his father, mother, brother and sister. As a 13-year-old it was bizarre to be with him, driving around and talking to me about this blackness in his life. We had never really spoken much until my brother left home. We certainly never had a close relationship, so why he felt it was so important that I knew these things was beyond me. It was only years later when I spoke to someone about my own abuse that our trip became personally significant.

My relationship with my dad was void of any consistency, emotional or otherwise. A week before my fifteenth birthday after getting back from the pub one night he made a random threat to kill someone whilst staring me dead in the eye. It freaked me out. It may just have been a passing comment without intention, or it may not have been. But I was in no mind to stick around to find out, he was too unpredictable.

A few days later I plucked up the courage to leave. I left early one morning, he was passed out drunk, half of him in the hallway and the other half in the living room stinking of booze. I walked out the door of my family home with nothing but fear and resentment in my heart and with no idea how to face life. All I took was my guitar and a small suitcase with a few clothes and books. I hated him for failing me, and from the day I left I never saw past my anger towards him and it affected everyone I would ever meet.

I was too young to understand that he had problems that stopped him from being close to me as his son. There were times he tried to bond with me but when he made effort with me it always felt uncomfortable. When he would take me out drinking, maybe that was his way of finding a connection with me. Drunk was the only time he was ever open enough to talk. Even our bizarre trip around Wales seemed in my mind to hint towards the hope we would meet somewhere on a father/son level. Looking back maybe it was something we both wanted to happen, but I resented him for his impatience and intolerance towards me. And for as long as I felt that way, he was damned if he tried and damned if he didn't. Anger destroyed both of us.

I stayed with friends and their families but was hard work. I already had problems with alcohol, add my erratic emotional state into the mix and I was a walking disaster. I slept rough from time to time when I was either drunk or causing trouble for the people who tried to help me out. The landlord of the local pub would leave his car unlocked so if I ever got stuck out in the rain, I at least had shelter. Sometimes I would hitch-hike to other towns and villages on the off chance of finding someone from school who could put me up for a night.

My mum left home shortly after me and stayed with friends in another town. I would hitch-hike to see her occasionally when I needed money. I didn't see my brother again for years and would never feel any close connection to my family for a long time. I resented them. I resented myself and my only relief was to drink.

*

My school days fizzled out as my attendance dropped. I Had also heard a rumour my dad was looking for me and was angry. He had been to friend's houses and I was told he said he would be waiting for me after school one day. The police got involved and an injunction order was put in place, legally he wasn't allowed anywhere near me. Still I didn't want to take the risk. I was terrified of him. So, at fifteen I left school with no qualifications. The only certificates to my name (and neither are framed and hanging on the wall) are achievements I collected in later years. One for completing eighteen gruelling months of dialectical behavioural therapy for borderline personality disorder. And the other one for white knuckling three months of sobriety in a drug and alcohol advisory group I was made to go to. Which I promptly celebrated with a bottle of rum after completing. At fifteen my life was already hampered by mental health problems and alcohol abuse as I struggled with depression and anxiety.

I quickly found work, I knew If I was going to drink, I would need money. A kind boss let me sleep in the attic of the workplace, and eventually let me live at his home with his wife. When the arrangement became a problem, he paid my deposit on a bedsit room and I moved into my first place. He also paid for a cheap old moped so I could get to work from the town I was living in. But I eventually burnt my bridges and lost the job. I was a loose cannon and unreliable. I also took liberties with those who helped me. I had a bad attitude towards life and people. And to put myself in the position of people who tried to help me out. How long can you go out of your way to help a kid who can't be helped? I drained people.

I went from job to job, never lasting long in new employment. My first suicide attempt happened at the age of Sixteen whilst in a drunk blackout, it would be the first of many. I also began losing my hair as a result of the stress I was experiencing. By Nineteen the internal pressure broke me, and I was hospitalised on a psychiatric ward suffering from the symptoms of paranoid schizophrenia. During my teens there was rarely a time I wasn't medicated or in therapy. My life became ever more self-absorbed and self-driven as I searched to find answers to my problems. I started to believe that if I had the right job, the right amount of money, the right people around me to supply the esteem I felt I deserved, the hollowness in me would be filled. That under the right circumstances I would find happiness and relief from the growing void within. As far as I was concerned the world owed me. I began to develop an irrational sense of entitlement, or "high self-esteem", an egotistical trait all alcoholics suffer from. The more fearful and resentful I felt towards life, the more selfish and self-centred I became.

I remained attached to a growing spirit of resentment with no clue of how to cope with every-day life and no real moral guidance. I got jobs that never lasted and lived in cheap dirty bedsits and spent any money I had on alcohol. I emulated the people I admired for their approval, drunks on barstools frequenting the pubs I drank in with their gassy mean stories of bravado and fast right hooks. They didn't seem to fear or care about anyone. And in my head, that's how I knew I had to be if I was going to survive in this world. My big secret was, as much of a front as I put on, under it all I was scared. I was a fraud and had no idea who I really was. The stresses of life, along with the stress of keeping up my phony image kept mounting and I kept stuffing the fear down. One day I would explode. It's how I ended up on a psychiatric ward. The symptoms of suppressing anger were punching through. (I later discovered my father had stayed on the same psychiatric ward, a few years prior to my own heavily medicated six-week assessment).

I did meet my dad again when I was eighteen. I met him in a pub one day and it was awkward for both of us. But we both made the effort to talk. He had met a woman in the psychiatric hospital who was terminally ill, and they married. We drank and didn't talk much about anything from the past. We arranged to meet again. The second time we met there was a tension in him. We had a few drinks and at one point I made a light joke at him, He looked me straight in the eye and growled "you and I are going to fall out again".

In that moment I lost any hope that we would have any sort of relationship. I felt fear and anger rise in me that threw me back to the last couple of years at home with him. I couldn't be around him. There was too much distance between us and too much anger tying us together. I picked up my drink, knocked it back and walked out the door. It was the last time I ever saw or heard from my dad again.

I continued to struggle with everyday life, personal relationships and poor mental health into my early twenties.

*

The only thing I felt I had going for me in life was my self-taught ability to play guitar and sing a few notes. I became obsessed with the fantasy that I was going be plucked from obscurity and placed on stage at Wembley stadium where I felt I rightly deserved to be. That fantasy was easier to live with than my reality. I fancied myself as a fast burning light like some of my hero's such as Jim Morrison and Kurt

Cobain who both died at the age of twenty-seven. On the night of my twenty-third birthday when it suddenly occurred to me that my dream was not going to materialise, I quickly sank into a deep depression. Already drunk I cracked open a litre bottle of vodka and starting chugging with a vengeance in the hope of not waking up. Obviously, it didn't work. Instead I woke up the following afternoon in a wet bed with wet pants and quadruple vision. My fantasy had been smashed and it was time again to re-evaluate where I was in life and try and make some changes. It was at that time I realised that if I wanted to get anywhere in life, I was going to have to work for it. I also learned a valuable lesson in that focusing my thoughts to get what I wanted in life doesn't work. It just pulls me further from the present moment and deeper into a phony fantasy land of existence.

At twenty-four I had a real shot at a normal life. I still drank but found a shred of management with it (at least I thought I did). I also seemed to have got my depression and paranoia under control by switching from prescribed medications such as antipsychotics to street drugs like ecstasy, speed and marijuana, I felt it a step in the right direction as I was no longer taking the doctors' orders and holding my own without the help of psychiatrists and the support of mental health teams. That and the drugs were far more agreeable to me. It was around that time I finally met someone who I fell in love with, and she loved me for who I was. We got married after a couple of years together. Brought a home which we soon rented out and both travelled a good chunk of the world together. My life changed drastically.

Whilst in Fiji, an opportunity to work in Australia materialized whilst drinking at a bar with a real character of an Irish man. It was a job that eventually came with a chance to live in Melbourne. So, when our travels ended, we sold our home in the U.K, packed everything up and moved to the other side of the world. For the first time in my life I was making good memories and great friend's, all tied in with some amazing experiences along the way. I was on an exhilarating ride and I loved it, fuelled of course by drink. By leaving the U.K It felt as though all my problems were also being left behind. It was the ultimate chance at a fresh start for my wife and me, and I started celebrating my new freedom the moment I got on the plane and stayed blackout drunk for days.

But there was a problem in that everywhere I went, I was always there! My thoughts, my fears and resentments were always bubbling under the surface like an angry infection I couldn't heal (along with the daily reminder from my overactive mind that I'm no good and was born evil). And no matter what I did to distract from those thoughts or stuff them down, they always surfaced and took the wheel. As hard as I tried, I failed to contain them. To drink was my only relief from the anxiety and anger I felt towards myself and others. Yet drinking was destroying everything good in my life.

My drinking took its toll quickly as I settled into life down under, there was a drinking culture that suited me down to the ground. I had discovered paradise, only with a hangover. But the pressures of work and marriage soon got too much as I failed to control my relationship with drink. I was losing touch with my wife and the friends I had made as my mental health began to decline. An overwhelming fear took hold when a friend suggested I slow down on the booze. My friends and work colleagues had growing concerns around me, the fear I felt was knowing that I was out of control.

The other re-occurring nightmare was that I knew I would let my wife down at some point. Either by cheating on her drunk or failing her simply because I was losing my mind. The party was over, and the initial excitement of moving had dissipated. Talk between us turned to settling down and I felt pressure to slow down, from work as well as from my wife. We were after all a married couple, both with good jobs and opportunities in front of us. It was here I got frightened. What if she got pregnant and we had a child? It would probably happen at some point. The idea of becoming a parent terrified me. I could barely take care of myself. Up until that point my wife had taken care of everything concerning bills and paperwork, balancing finances and anything that involved organisation. I was totally clueless in those areas of everyday life. I always felt it was my job to bring a bottle, a good time and keep the party fuelled. I had always felt that was a fair and equal balance as a couple working together. To say she was the brains of the operation would be an understatement. To bring a child into the world that I would have to step up to with responsibility and take care of was a threat to my self-centred existence, that threat was only alive through the fear of my inability to be stable. Emotionally or otherwise. It would be a potential disaster for all involved, I would never be what they need from me.

These fears rapidly culminated into a drastic decision on my part, I had to leave my wife before I hurt her or any babies came along, I felt cornered and saw it as the only option for her future wellbeing knowing full well the downward slope I was on. One day I came home from work and told her out of the blue that I couldn't go on with her anymore, that I didn't love her, and the marriage was over. I gave no other explanation for my actions. She was speechless. I left the house, walked to the off licence at the end of the street and grabbed a bottle of whisky. Then got in a taxi to go to a friend's house. When I got in the cab I broke down. I felt like the lowest, most cowardly piece of shit on earth. I hated what I did to her that day. No-one deserves to be treated that way. I had no interest in trying to make it work as she later suggested, or to try marriage counselling to work through my problems. I was on a path of self-destruction, and the less people involved the better. My drinking stepped up a notch from its already destructive pace after I walked out on my wife. I had to drown the guilt of my actions. It would be years before I made my amends to her. She had spent the years following blaming herself for our divorce as she had no other explanation from me as to why I left. She couldn't move on from the hurt. She told me it felt like I died one day and just wasn't there anymore.

It was just one of many personal relationships that I walked away from because I didn't know how to settle and do life. I knew how to start a relationship, I just didn't have what it took to stay with someone and go the distance through the ups and downs that life brings, when I felt any pressure it was always easier to leave. I was the guy with one foot out of the door no matter what the situation I was in because self-reliance as a rule, always failed me. I have done many selfish things in my time, but nothing more hurtful than how I treated a woman who did nothing but love and care about me.

Chapter 3

Dangerous obsessions

I boarded the plane at Melbourne en route to the South Island of New Zealand. Walking away from what was supposed to be a fresh start in Australia. Instead it was over and now I was leaving an abusive violent relationship that had begun a few months prior in an alcohol and drug detox clinic. From the day I arrived in Australia my drinking and mental health spiralled out of control. A few months after I walked out on my marriage, and with my job on the rocks my bosses sent me into a drying out clinic to get help. I resented them deeply for that. I felt they were making an example out of me. The reality was they were taking care of me at a time I was unable to help myself, but I was far too absorbed in my problems and obsessive drinking to see it.

Whilst in the clinic, high on Valium and detoxing from alcohol I met a girl (not the best environment to find love) and we had a dream that we would find sobriety together and live a happy life. I wanted it more than anything in my insane state and believed she wanted the same. But with alcoholism in the mix and no way of staying sober when we left the safety of the hospital there was a clear absence of stability, and through that lack of emotional balance came an inability to care for each other. I was quickly tied to her only by anger, jealousy and bitterness. Our relationship was nothing more than violent outbursts, sex and rare moments of clarity where we would talk about better days ahead. It was a train-wreck that I struggled to walk away from. Yet after a serious violent incident in which I was hospitalised, and she was arrested I had no choice but to leave the country.

On the plane I struggled to get comfortable in the small seat. Although the stab wounds had almost healed, the muscle tissue in my back, abdomen and arm was bruised and ached. It took effort and concentration to click up the seatbelt. The recent surgery I had on my wrist after accidentally slashing it open punching a window out in a drunken rage had been successful in reattaching the tendons, but my hand was weak and my fingers difficult to move. I was told by a physio it would be at least another eight months before I gained any real strength back in my hand and that it would always be numb. This bothered me as I would need to find work when I landed in New Zealand. I was running out of money and had to start from scratch again. I had no plan when I got there. I didn't know anyone. I had a one-way ticket and just needed to start again where no-one knew me. I was in bad shape.... again.

As I watched the ground fall beneath me, I felt anger

frustration and guilt. My life had fallen apart again. Every willful decision I made seemed to boomerang and come crashing down on me, yet I had no other way of going through life. I just did the next thing that I thought was right for me with the best intentions, oblivious to the self-centredness of my wants and needs.

I found it hard to take in that eighteen months prior to boarding that flight, I had landed in Australia from the U.K with a good job, a wife, friends who respected me and a world of opportunity at my feet. Now I was leaving alone with a suitcase and a guitar. Just a straight up drunken angry mess. It wasn't the first time I had left somewhere after dramatically burning all my bridges down to start over. Except now it was different. I was running out of drive. I was a thirty-year old man who had failed at managing my life, my marriage, personal relationships my erratic emotions and now drinking.

As I sat on that flight, I felt a rising guilt that was making me increasingly uncomfortable. I was sobering up. For me there was nothing worse than having to look at myself. And without anything in my system, and nothing to distract my racing mind all I had was me. And I hated what I had become.

After warnings from the friends who had gone out of their way to make me feel welcomed and a part of their lives, I had failed to stay sober on my own. It was the first time in my life my drinking had been exposed as problematic by people I cared about, at least to the point it bothered me. I had let those closest to me down again and felt guilty and frustrated. With the reality check of my inability to control my drinking came a painful realisation. I had to stop. I already knew I couldn't by that point but there was another fear rising in me around sobriety - that I would have to live with my mind and somehow deal with life. With the constant barrage of negative thinking, the pounding fears and agitations I experienced without the alcohol in my system that drowned out the noise and the pain so well. Sobriety was a grey area for me. There was no brightness or joy in that place. Just depression, paranoia and darkness. How anyone could live that way was beyond me. I grew to dislike sober people, mostly because they had the key to something I didn't. Nothing pissed me off more than everyday normal people doing normal everyday things. I resented the hell out of them. The truth was it was my inability to live a normal life that I resented so much.

As I gazed out the window these thoughts and fears swirled around my sobering mind, I was getting agitated and wracked with guilt. I made the decision in that moment to quit drinking......... Just not right then. I was getting sick and needed a heart-starter. I ordered a few vodkas to help pick me up and with that hit of alcohol came that drive of pure self-will. My guilt washed down and my arrogance returned with gusto as I heard once again the cries of bravado from the barstools with the heat of the alcohol rising from my belly to my head. And with that almost instant inflation of my ego I knew exactly what I had to do. Pick myself up and start again. Screw the world and everyone in it and if they didn't like it, they could go to hell! I wasn't going to drown in self-pity! And just maybe, I might quit drinking down the line when I get a few of my other more pressing problems resolved.

*

During my time in New Zealand I went downhill quickly. I got a job and managed to live from week to week. There were regular visits to A & E from injuries sustained while drunk, or from getting beaten up. I also returned to visit the girl I couldn't let go of back in Australia, I was still hanging on to the idea we might make it somehow. I was stopped by the police when I got through passport control and taken into a side room to be questioned as to why I had returned after the incident I was involved in before I left. Maybe they thought I had come back to cause trouble or get revenge. I explained I was visiting and staying with my girlfriend to which one of the three police officers looked at me confused and asked, "Mate why are you here to visit a girl who stabbed you?". My answer, "because I love her". And in my twisted mind I did. She was all I had left in the world. They told me I was crazy and had to let me go. And the truth is I was - crazy.

It was an ugly time. Nothing had changed between us, if anything we had only gotten worse. There were no moments of clarity or talk of the future anymore, just drunkenness and fuelled anger. The last few days of my stay I somehow managed to avoid an aggravated assault charge after a drunken incident that would have seen me in prison had the man gone ahead and pressed charges. I knew I had to walk away from it all in Melbourne and let her go. Any hope of a future together had been snuffed out. It was too dangerous a relationship, and the truth were if had it carried on any longer one, or both of us would have ended up dead.

It was one of the more sensible decisions I had made in a long while. Yet walking away from her was one of the hardest things I had ever done. The emotional pain of letting her go with her threats of suicide, and my obsession to fix her in the broken mental state I was in was too much for me to deal with when I got back to New Zealand. My train had finally derailed.

I couldn't go on anymore. My fears were eating me alive and I was faced with two choices, either take my own life and make it all stop. Not just for me but for the pain I was causing others like my Mum, who had flown out to visit me in New Zealand during my last months of drinking and reported to the family when she arrived home that they wouldn't see me again.

The other option than suicide was to try to get sober and attempt to live the way I feared the most. It took me seven months from first arriving in New Zealand before I finally threw the towel in with alcohol. I was Fifteen pounds under weight, I couldn't string a coherent sentence together. I was hallucinating and suicidal. There was no one left in my life that I could turn to and my drinking had burnt me out in every way. There was no direction left to go. I was done.

I sat in tears on the dirty mattress on the floor of the little room I rented. I have never felt so defeated, beaten and ashamed of myself. And there was no-one left to blame but me, and that's what hurt the most. Self was the problem - I was the problem and I couldn't avoid that truth anymore.

There had to be a solution to my internal conflicts, and by that, I mean living with the feeling of permanent dread, agitation and anger. The constant judging of others that created guilt in me. The creeping feeling something was not right. An ever-present sense of darkness under my skin I was unable to explain and had battled with continually in my mind since childhood. A conflict that caused me to sabotage everything good in my life. I was convinced that alcohol wasn't really my problem, to me it had been the sole solution that carried me through life. It supplied me with the way I wanted to feel. Most importantly It blotted out my consciousness, the one thing I ran from that would eventually be my saving grace.

Chapter 4

Searching for a solution

So began my search. Firstly, for a solution to my alcoholism, and as important for a way to face, and live with the pressures of life and the conflicts within myself. I needed to find a new way to live. I sought a solution for my drinking that night at a meeting of a worldwide spiritual fellowship of recovered alcoholics. I was aware these people existed as I was made to go to meetings in the drying out Clinic back in Melbourne. I had shunned them off back then as a bunch of delusional nut cases who talked about higher powers and abstinence and I wasn't signing up for any of that crap! But I knew there were meetings everywhere. And as I discovered when I moved into the dilapidated house I was then residing in, by some bizarre universal chance there just happened to be a meeting held in the community cottage next door. A meeting that I had walked into during my first week when arriving on the South Island and promptly walked out of to go and get drunk after being reminded they were all crazy. Before I left that meeting though, a woman called Jennifer gave me an old thick blue book to read. She told me it was all about recovering from alcoholism and that I had to return it the following week as it was important to the group and had been in that meeting for years. Of course, I didn't go back, and the groups fond relic of a book got stuffed in the bottom of my suitcase and forgotten about until the night I finally did go back. I used the returning of the book as an excuse to go to the meeting, I was dying of alcoholism but still had a deep reluctance to go.

When I walked through the door in my stinking beaten-up state with scraggy blue hair and dirty clothes, a man walked up to me smiling and asked if I lived next door, I told him I did. He then laughed and told me they wondered when they would see me in the meeting on account of all the empty spirit and beer bottles that overflowed from the recycling boxes out by the kerb. The meeting was full of kind people who welcomed me, not least the woman who had lent me the book who was overjoyed to see me again. I sat in tears through the entire meeting and never took in a single word that anyone said. All I knew about this place was that the solution they had was spiritual in nature. At the end of the meeting an old heavy built man who looked like he spent his life in the boxing ring approached me, I thought he might have wanted to punch me in the face in my paranoid state. Instead he put his hand out to shake mine, looked me dead in the eye and with a look of kind concern said "Son, I suggest you start praying". It was the weirdest thing anyone had said to me. But that night I did.

I began going to regular meetings but failed to stay sober for more than a few days at a time. I would just get angry or filled with fear and need to pick up a drink. I got overwhelmed by the different suggestions and advice I was given as I ducked in and out of a fellowship that only confused me as to what I was supposed to do. Some said I had to stay sober by going to meetings for the rest of my life and sharing my problems. That just sounded to me like therapy which I already knew didn't work. Talking to another person is a good thing, it can alleviate some of the pain, but spending my life reliant on sitting in church basements spewing my problems out to others didn't sound much like the freedom from alcoholism I heard some mention. There were people who spoke of a personal connection with God they had found through the Twelve step program this fellowship offered. And there were folks telling me to stay away from the "God people" because they were nuts. Some said I needed to go into treatment and others said treatment was a waste of time. In short, I spent three months struggling to understand how I was going to get, and more importantly remain sober. I quickly grew resentful of the only real hope I had left.

One morning I snapped out of a blackout while walking along a street after a bender. At a guess by the area I was in

I had been in the Chinese brothel. After calling into work to explain I was a bit sick and wouldn't be in that day, I made my way to the casino with what money I had left in my pocket. The security man was adamant that they didn't want my presence in their fine establishment and asked me in so many words to "go away". After firmly letting him know what I thought of him and his shoddy place of employment, I went to get the drink I was in dire need of. As I sat by the river slugging back red wine, I began to sink into a dark realisation. The fellowship that was supposed to hold the key to my freedom from alcoholism was a waste of time. I didn't get it, or maybe I was too far gone to be helped. Either way they needed to know how I felt, so when Twelve o'clock came I stumbled into a lunch time meeting. It was big, there were probably thirty people in the room. I was in as bad a state as usual. After the formalities I put my hand up to speak and proceeded to tell them that I didn't get it, that there was something different about me and that as much as I was grateful to the kindness of the members that I was not coming back. I stood up, walked out of the silent room, you could have heard a pin drop as I waked out an emotional wreck and left the building. And the only thought I had was to go and end it all for good.

I stumbled out into the hot mid-day sun. As I walked away from the building someone came up from behind and stopped me in the middle of the street. I instantly recognised her as Jennifer, the kind woman who had lent me the groups old book from the first meeting I went to. She was also one of those "God people" I was told by some to stay away from. She wasted no time in asking me straight, "Are you done (drinking)? Have you had enough and are you willing to go to any lengths for your sobriety?"

Clearing the tears from my eyes and snot bubbles from my nose I told her I was. She continued, "I have been watching you since the day you came in, you're a dead man walking. I can help you, but you need to be willing to follow a set of clear-cut directions. And nothing can ever come between you and what you must do to stay sober. Are you ready to do this? "

I had a vague idea of what she was asking of me from what I'd heard in the meetings and replied, "I am".

Then came the bombshell "Are you willing to believe that there is a power greater than yourself that can solve your problem?".

It was a question I had asked myself over and over since finding this spiritual fellowship as it was a requirement in recovering from alcoholism, but in the bad shape I was in I didn't hesitate, I had nothing left to lose, I answered "Yes, I am".

She made a quick phone call before returning her attention

back to me. "I have a couple of friends who will be here in about ten minutes. They'll take care of you for the rest of the day and will safely get you sober. Tomorrow morning I'll be at your house at 10 am and you will make a start on the 12-step recovery program this fellowship offers. Be there and don't waste my time".

And as she had organised, two men who I had never met pulled up, told me to get in the car and we drove off. I was half terrified of the verbal agreement I had just made with that formidable woman, a quarter drunk and a quarter in fear these guys were axe murderer's and I was their next victim. We drove miles out of town to visit a man they were helping to get sober. This young man had recently got out of prison and was talking about his faith and how since finding sobriety his outlook on life had changed, and how he was now happily raising his son. From there we went to another house back in the city to a couple who were helping another man find sobriety, giving him a place to stay. They cooked up a meal for me and loaded me with sugary drinks and orange juice to help with my physical shaking as I detoxed. The whole day these men and women who had years of permanent sobriety took care of me, just to see I got through the day alive. They looked after a total stranger they knew nothing about, without judgment of me and wanting nothing in return. They talked all day about a power greater than themselves that had done the impossible and granted them freedom from drinking. They talked about God but were not religious, they had personal experiences with personal stories. They helped me because they too had suffered from alcoholism and understood the gravity and the hopelessness of my situation. I had spent my life sniggering and laughing at people of faith, judging them for believing the way they did. So, it was a humbling experience, knowing that if that selfless woman of faith had not followed me out of the meeting that day. It would have been my last day on this earth. She saved my life.

Jennifer helped me as she said she would. And It was then I began to understand alcoholism, which itself is just a set of two symptoms. A mental obsession which was beyond my control, coupled with a physical craving which I always experienced once I put alcohol in my system. It explained my utter lack of control and inability to leave it alone.

I took a half honest hard look at myself for the first time in my life and it was an ugly sight. I had no idea how much of a self-centred man I had become. Everything I did was motivated by a need to serve myself. I was as honest as I felt I needed to be with her about everything that caused my resentments and fears but held on to something that I swore I would never tell a soul. That I was born evil and the memories I had from sexual abuse. Although through-out my life it was my biggest roadblock to ever knowing a moments peace and was the instigator of most of my mental health problems (I say most, because many of my problems I created myself). I couldn't bring myself to unburden myself of it. I still had so much fear, guilt and shame around it. In short it was just too painful to bring up. It was easier to keep that information about myself stuffed deep down, so that's what I did. I had given Jennifer my word I would be completely honest with her, and I wasn't. It was however the first time I saw myself in a new light and became aware of what needed to change if I was to live a new life that wasn't completely focused on me.

One day Jennifer took me for a drive to visit a hillside spot with a little bench and a breath-taking view of the Southern Alps. It was a place she went to find peace and quiet from time to time. The snow-capped mountains stretching out in the distance is a view I will never forget. Whilst on that hillside, I made the decision to ask for help from something I barely believed in. I didn't know anything about faith or God but was desperate, I was terrified of drinking, and of facing a life of abstinence from alcohol. What followed became one of the most pivotal moments of my life. I said a childlike prayer and asked for help.

I don't have the words to describe what happened in the next moment. It was an experience that I couldn't explain. Jen was aware of it too. And even though I was heading back into trouble and madness because I didn't really understand the underlying spiritual cause of my problems, from that day on I never again questioned the existence of something bigger than me in this universe. A power outside of me that I was yet to understand. My perception on life also began to change from that moment.

Jen allowed me to stay with her so I could move out of the dilapidated old place I was living in and focus on my recovery. She warned me almost daily that getting sober wasn't enough. That I had to grow in the principles of love, patience and tolerance with others and it would be a lifetime job. That it was prayer and meditation that held the key to this growth. She had a faith that didn't waver. When I asked her why she went out of her way to help me she told me the story of a young man who was in and out of those meetings just before I turned up, who was in bad shape like I was. People offered him money and advise but little else. One day they found his dead body in a ditch. She said I reminded her of him, and although she had fears around helping me because of my angry mental state she put her faith in God to keep her safe and asked for all she needed to help me. And because no-one else was stepping in, in her heart she knew that If no one else offered me help I would go the same way as that young man. She told me that when I recovered myself, she hoped I would do the same for others, and never to turn my back on an alcoholic that sincerely wants a solution.

I didn't know anything about God or had cared much to understand up until my rock bottom in New Zealand. All I knew though was that if others didn't have faith and trust in a power greater than themselves, I would have never got back to England. I learned from her actions a lesson in selfless love for another human being, no matter how far they have fallen. A lesson I will never forget.

Chapter 5

The final round

I returned to England thanks to a tax rebate that arrived unexpectedly from my previous employment in Australia, which just about covered the cost of a flight back. I stepped off the plane at Heathrow with eight New Zealand dollars, a few clothes and a guitar. I was ready to start again with a new attitude towards life but instantly met a few hurdles. I was unable to open a bank account because I didn't have a fixed address, nor could I claim any benefits because I had been out of the country.

I moved back in with my mum at her place of work but within months I was drunk and back in hospital after another suicide attempt whilst in a blackout. Although I'd had an experience on a hillside that sparked a change in my consciousness, I gradually grew resentful, fearful, obsessive and overwhelmed with my thinking again. It seemed I had found a way to stop drinking temporarily - it was staying sober and emotionally stable that became the real challenge I faced. The solution to ongoing sobriety and emotional consistency was pointing towards meditation. Once the obsession to drink was removed, I had to somehow remain conscious of rising fears and anger within myself and stay free from it – letting it go as it cropped up rather than stuffing it down inside me. Yet it was here I found my biggest hurdle. I didn't know anything about meditation and no-one else seemed much the wiser. I discovered there are literally thousands of practices on offer. Most of them unhelpful distraction technics mainly based around Buddhist mindfulness and other Eastern religious practices.

I moved to a remote island off the north of Scotland in the Orkney isles after my drunken episode. It was an opportunity to spend time in solitude, far from the distractions of normal life. The only reason that move came about was because Jen, back in New Zealand, knowing I was again struggling with alcohol contacted a couple she knew of living on an island. Who as it turned out, were looking for someone to do some temporary work on their old cottage and surrounding acres. I was warned before I arrived that if I drank, I would be on the first plane off the island.

It was another fresh start in another new place where no-one knew me. I always saw those geographical escapes as opportunities to begin again. To build from the most recent wreckage behind me. And I did - for while at least. I stayed with strangers who quickly became friends and with no money worked for my lodgings and meals. I worked hard, seven days a week doing building work, landscaping and whatever I was asked to do. Before long I was asked by other residence of the tiny island to do building maintenance jobs for them. I learned how to do the work required from watching you tube video's and asking questions on tradesmen forums. I became a valued hard-working member of the community.

Eventually I was given the opportunity of permanent steady employment rebuilding an old Crofters cottage with one of the resident builders on the island, who has remained a good friend to this day. Along with the offer came the chance to live in my own furnished house. It was small but had all I needed.

All I did was work and play guitar, constantly distracting from my overactive mind. It was a paradise escape from the pressures of the real world. If I could have stayed there forever, I would have. Because I didn't have to deal with life's complications. But I was aware that island life wasn't going to last forever and became anxious at the thought of leaving. That fear grew as the work came to an end. I needed to get back to the mainland U.K, I was hiding from life and It wasn't the place for a single young man to stay.

During my time on the island I began practicing a guided meditation that had me placing all my worries in a box and visualising them floating away each night with the idea of clearing my mind of my negativity. Not surprisingly it didn't work. The practiced suggested I had the power within myself to solve my anxieties and restlessness by way of my imagination (my ego loved the idea I held this sort of power). Instead It pulled me further into thoughts, and deeper into playing God and struggling with my fears around leaving the island. And as was becoming apparent to me - If I had the power within myself to solve my problems and face life successfully it would have happened long before then. I grew more frustrated and angrier below the surface during the last months. I began self-harming, and fantasy thoughts of suicide became focal points of relief. A couple of drunken episodes concerned the other islanders as I got overwhelmed with my thinking and anxieties towards the end of my stay. The meditation I had committed to brought me the opposite effect of delivering calmness and a solution to the negative energy I was experiencing. I had arrived in the Orkney islands with the best intentions. And a year later I was leaving full of fear and resentment at myself for failing to find emotional sobriety.

The kind islanders came to wave me off as I boarded the little eight-seater propeller plane to the mainland. I watched the tiny snow-covered paradise escape disappear behind me, sat in discomfort from the deep cuts I had given myself while trying to bring relief from the angry thinking that was consuming me that previous week. I was deflated and beaten and heading back into the real world again with all my problems – and I was thirsty. Really fucking thirsty!

I went for a drink after checking into the hotel on the mainland, just to relax! My plane was leaving for the south of England that following morning so I figured a few drinks to take the edge off wouldn't do any harm. I had amounted to a pressure cooker of agitation and fear and needed instant relief. My next conscious moment I was being woken up in a police cell to speak to a psychiatrist for an assessment before release. I had no clue as to why I was in there. I vaguely remember feeding him some bullshit story that would get me out of being hospitalised, and it worked. Slightly smug at my ability to outwit a psychiatrist while still half-drunk from the night before I was promptly escorted to the airport. The two police officers who drove me made sure I boarded the flight back to the south of England. I stayed drunk after that day for another three months before checking into a detox.

The visualisation meditation had failed me, as did my ongoing attempts at self-management. And the problem I faced was that most of the meditations I got introduced to were of the same thing. Offering distraction and suppression from my racing mind. Almost as if pretending the problems don't exist, that through fantasising or distracting away from reality I could resolve my internal spiritual malady. It used to be called psychosis. Now it seems there is a market for it. Yet I naively bought into these easily available and dangerous practices without any understanding of the effects they would have. I know from my experiences now that no meditation practice is a toy. They can all have serious spiritual consequences.

That drink sparked the beginning of more mental health diagnosis', more therapy and more counselling. And worst of all back on antipsychotic medications mixed with spells of alcohol and drug use. This was my path for the next five years. I was losing hope again of a normal life. I needed help, but no-one seemed to have the answer to the emotional sobriety I craved. If I could face life and the stresses that came with it, I knew I would be okay. But it was slipping out of my reach. My own thinking was continually against me as I battled with paranoia and depression. I became obsessed with the idea that I would one day control my drinking. It was my last hope, as a normal life of sobriety seemed impossible for someone like me with the problems I had.

I was kindly housed in a council flat after being registered homeless, supported by a mental health team. I spent my last days of drinking in that flat. I had found work but was on my final warning for not turning up. Paranoid without drink and anxious with it I was a mess. It no longer brought me the relief and freedom from my own head as it once did. I had spent five years fighting to stay sober without finding any permanent relief.

I poured my last drink on a Sunday morning. A rum and

coke. My flat stank of stale tobacco and marijuana smoke as the sun broke through the crack in the curtains, illuminating the lines of haze. My head raced, unable to focus on a single thought I didn't even bother to try and drown out my mind with music. I just sat in the silence. I picked up the glass and stared at the black liquid inside. It used to be the party starter, it used to give me freedom from myself and my troubles. It used to be the answer. But as I swirled it around, rising it to the rim of the glass I got punched with a horrible and deflating realisation. It was never going to work for me again, I desperately wanted it to, but knew that it was over. This wasn't the rock bottom I had reached in NZ. This was on a deeper level with all the understanding I now had of myself and with six years of failing to recover.

I knew as I stared at the glass that I was never going to be the man who enjoyed and controlled his drinking, as much as I'd tried. I was always going to be the weak selfish bastard that ran away from life. The biggest realisation that floored me on that morning was that the pain of sobriety was all I had left, and it crushed me. I was at a rock bottom on an emotional level like I had never experienced. As I got overwhelmed with a sense of defeat my mind threw up memories of the people I'd hurt. The memories of my childhood still haunted me every day. I couldn't shut off the guilt I felt around the people I had used to prop up my selfish existence and had let down over the years. I had made promises to my mum that I would stay sober, instead I now struggled to look her in the eye. She was exhausted from worry. From a lifetime of watching me crash and burn. She had to watch the child she loved grow up and destroy himself just as his father had. I loathed what I had become. I was nothing - left with nothing and everything in me was broken and I didn't know how to fix it and it hurt so much. I wanted to end it all there and then - for good.

I fell to my knees and the pain in my chest was burning into my throat as I cried in absolute shame. I prayed for help - for forgiveness. I didn't know what else to do. I could no longer go on. There was a void in me I couldn't fill and a darkness within me I couldn't shake, if there was a God, I needed him now more than ever.

I had a powerful spiritual experience that left me anxious and shaken. It frightened me. And as I eventually got off my knees It physically felt that something in me was gone, was no longer present. My obsession to drink left me that morning and I have never touched another drop of alcohol since. And the thought has never crossed my mind to do so. Something had inexplicably changed and with that supernatural awakening came a massive shift in my consciousness. I once heard a man say the hounds of heaven will chase you right into the gates of hell. After that spiritual liberation in my flat I finally understood what he meant. For years my scepticism around God was driven by the thought that if there was a God, why was there so much suffering in the world? I came to realise the answer to that question is because there is an electric force of darkness (resentment/fear) that exists, as well as force of light (love and truth). Two opposing forces that as spiritual beings we attract and cannot avoid. Darkness works through emotions and feeds the ego, and light comes through consciousness and is a guiding force of love. It was only when I was completely willing to let go of the darkness I had seen in myself, that I experienced light. And It wasn't an experience that happened to me from studying books, going to church every week, becoming religious or forcing it to happen through sheer self-will. There were no requirements or effort that contributed, just a personal spiritual brokenness that I recognised and a desperate willingness to allow something outside of myself to heal what I couldn't.

It left me with an overwhelming sense that everything was going to be okay. And I knew that if I could hang on to whatever it was that had just happened to me, I had finally found the solution to my biggest problem. My whole perception on life and my place in the world changed from that day. I take no personal credit for recovering from alcoholism. None what-so-ever.

Two months later I met Stacey, who would become my wife.

Chapter 6

Emotional consistency and new beginnings

To introduce you to Stacey I need to take you back a few years to the island.

When I first moved to the Orkneys, I lived in a static caravan behind "Shore house", the aptly named quaint stone cottage I was helping to work on. The small stone house was built next to a reef, and the edge of the garden dropped straight onto a pure white sandy beach that curved away like a horseshoe. The water in the that bay was turquoise in colour and crystal clear in the long summer months. If there was the odd palm tree sticking up here and there instead of sheep and cows you could have easily imagined you were on a beach in the south pacific, rather than being in the middle of the cold north Atlantic Ocean.

I would walk my friend's rowdy little dog, who had got quite attached to me along the white sand in the mornings and the seals would follow us, bobbing up through the still water of the bay that sat between us and the small uninhabited island across from our beach. Curious of the barking dog that was clearly letting them know who was boss!

Those were times I would pray to maintain the sanity and calm I felt on those cold morning walks. At that time in my life I was beginning to think I would never be able to maintain a loving relationship with a woman. Whilst on the island I finally contacted my ex-wife to make my amends with her. She deserved an explanation of why I walked through the door from work one day and out of the blue told her I couldn't be with her anymore. Our marriage was over as fast as that. I didn't want to do anything of the things she suggested to try and save what we had because I knew I would let her down no matter what. With no real explanation from me as to why I had left she told me she felt as though I had died. I just left her and didn't look back. Because that's what I did in life, when the pressures of life mount, I run. It was a horrible way to treat someone I loved and to finally speak with her, and to see how much emotional damage I had caused was a deeply painful experience. After which I swore to myself, I would never be so cowardly to treat someone that way ever again.

If I was ever to be in a relationship that would work, I would have to be honest from the start and remain that way. I couldn't go into another one with a created phony image of myself that I would then tirelessly have to try and uphold. I was full of flaws and shortcomings that I refused to acknowledge, yet judged others for their imperfections. I had a skewed perception of how life and people should be, and it was all I could see. But I now had the fear that any woman in her right mind who really got to know me with my mental health problems, my alcoholism and the way I had treated others would never give me a second look. I was damaged goods. I didn't want to live my life alone but didn't really know what love was.

I knew a relationship was supposed to be about giving, and I could do that. The problem was I resented when I didn't get back what I felt I deserved. Whether it be attention, sex or otherwise. No-one ever met the expectations I put on them, and because of this selfish need of wanting what I felt was mine, then growing bitter for not getting what I thought I deserved, I was never happy. When I was that teenager full of anger and fear and decided the world owed me. I realised on that beach that I had never moved away from that thinking. I had to change but with all the self-absorbed thinking and fears in my head I had no idea how I was supposed to do that.

One morning I walked the yappy little dog along the stretch of sand the same as any other day. It was bright and still as the sun warmed the air. No clouds were in the sky and for some reason I felt compelled to stop and ask for some help to let go of the concerns that were bothering me. I stopped, closed my eyes and said a prayer, it went something like this.

"God, if you are out there and listening, I know I have fucked everything up until this point in all my relationships and have let so many people down. But maybe one day you could forgive me and help me be well enough to be in a healthy loving relationship that I can be selfless in, and to find a woman who will accept me for everything I am. And please give me the courage to be honest with her. Amen".

And I didn't worry or think again about Finding love. Because I intuitively knew that when the time was right, and I was well enough to have something to give to a relationship, it would happen. In God's time, not mine.

*

Now fast forward a few years, just two months after the spiritual experience I had in my flat I met Stacey. A woman with her feet on the ground who was raising a daughter on her own. I knew I was never going to drink again, and that I finally had discovered a new stability. I really liked her, she was a woman who clearly didn't take any shit and was beautiful to boot. We had been talking on the phone for a couple of weeks and had established a connection. We hadn't yet met, but I felt it was time to be honest with her. About my past and about my alcoholism. I felt it only right she should have the choice to continue giving me her time. She may just have seen me as a ticking time bomb and called it a day which I would have completely understood.

Before I made the call, I had that prayer in my head from the day on the beach. I knew if she accepted me, she was the one. I was a little nervous as she answered the phone. We said our usual hello's and I then proceeded to explain to her. "Stacey, I have a life-time behind me of wrecked relationships, alcoholism, drug use and mental health problems. I have only recently found permanent sobriety, and I can honestly say I will never drink again, and I no longer suffer from mental health problems. I have been completely honest with you up until now and feel you have the right to know the truth of my past. But If we are to continue you need to understand that nothing or no-one, including you, can come between me and my relationship with God, and the things I need to do to stay sober and emotionally well. Because without those things I will have nothing to offer, and I will only let you down"

I wasn't a religious man, and my faith was personal to me. So, to hear myself saying these things to a normal girl was a gamble. She would either hang up on me and I would never hear from her again. Or she wouldn't. There was what felt like an eternal pause before she responded "Yeah that's fine. You do what you need to do".

When I got off the phone to her, I knew without a doubt she was the one. I said another little prayer before I went to bed that night, it simply went "Thank you".

*

It was in a spirit of honesty that I got together with Stacey and stepped up to the role of a father figure in Frankie's life. Rather than go into another relationship to see what I could take. If I could put their needs ahead of my own and practice patience and tolerance above all else, then I could maybe bring something to their lives that would benefit them. In return my reward would be the opportunity to be the man I should have been from the start, before resentment and fear changed my path. One who could be relied on and who didn't run as soon as the pressures of life began to mount.

My first real experience of parenting with any conscious regard to what I was doing began with my stepdaughter Frankie.

From first meeting Stacey, we both felt it appropriate to wait before I was introduced to her daughter. When Frankie was three, they both went through an experience no family should have to endure. Stacey lost her partner, and Frankie lost her Dad to suicide. And although Frankie had no memory of the event, the emotional damage had stayed with her. She didn't need to deal with anymore disappointment If my relationship with Stacey was not going to work. Only when it became clear that Stacey and I had a real chemistry and decided to begin a commitment, I then met Frankie.

Becoming a father figure to Frankie was a big role to step into. I had a mass of responsibility and knew it. From me it took patience and vigilance to watch out for my own worries and fears that would crop up. There were times it was difficult to hear how much she wished her 'real dad' was still around. It was only my ego being dented, and there was no place for pride in our relationship. If I began harbouring secret childish resentments and fears towards her it would only damage her. I was the grown up. She had every right to express her feelings towards her biological father in any way she needed to. A demonstration of my patience and understanding was all she would need from me to be able to process her grief and maintain a trusting relationship with me.

She began calling me daddy further down the road on the day Stacey and I wed, which I made sure Frankie was a special part of. Known only to me, my mother-in-law and the minister, I had a ring made for her and vows written which during the wedding ceremony I read to Frankie before asking her If I could be her Dad. I promised to do my best, with God as my guide to love and take care of until the day I died. She accepted, and I have never let her down to this day. Even if somewhere down the line my marriage to Stacey didn't work out for whatever reason, I would still treat Frankie as my daughter.

It wasn't long before Frankie began to come out of her shell and find her strengths. She has grown into a confident, kind and caring little girl. it took a dedication to invest my time into that relationship. Just to listen, and give encouragement was enough to make a beginning. I had to stay aware of my own fears and doubts around parenting rather than let them become a wedge in our relationship, which was just as important to me as my relationship with her mum.

That first year with Stacey and Frankie became proof that the principles of love, patience and tolerance could be the foundation for a thriving home. No matter what our living arrangements or financial situation may be. I have seen first-hand and experienced myself the damaging affect the absence of a father can have on a child, whether he is at home or not. I also now know the confidence and stability a man can bring to a home when he is fully conscious and present.

*

Once again though at a year sober, I began to get the grating feeling that something wasn't right. I got lost again in different mindfulness meditations to try and hang on the awakened state of consciousness I had been granted a year before. It seemed that my spiritual experience was wearing off and I was slipping backwards. It scared me as now I had

Stacey and Frankie relying on me. I was getting agitated at everything. At every turn to ask for advice or help I was told the same thing. That anger is a normal healthy emotion and that I wasn't managing it properly or worrying over nothing. This got me more frustrated. I had worked hard to be a good parent to Frankie and a good partner to Stacey. Yet now I was becoming obsessed with my negative thinking and getting lost in the fear that my mental health was deteriorating again. As I became more and more attached to my thinking, so my agitation became harder to contain.

I was awake at night, my head buzzing. I couldn't sleep with all the negative thoughts coursing through my head. I was snapping at work colleagues and at home I had little patience. Something had to be done, I just didn't know what. I was backsliding into my old thinking and behaviours and if that happened, I would lose the two people I cared about the most.

I went back to the spiritual fellowship in search of someone with answers. I had to wade through the amateur therapists, whose frothy suggestions such as writing gratitude lists every night and doing activities that distracted me from my agitations were never going to be of real help. I eventually found a man through a social media site who introduced himself as a recovered alcoholic. He offered a solution by way of a meditation which immediately got my back up.

After first contacting this stranger by email I got angry at him for pointing out some truths about why I was failing, he wasn't being horrible, I was just so angry and defensive I couldn't see past myself to take in anything he was saying. And I was never going to get in touch with the bastard again! I mean who the hell does this guy think he is being honest with me?

Thankfully my wife, aware of the backslide I was in, and who was now watching me pace around the house full of agitation, mumbling expletives under my breath asked me what he had said that pissed me off so much. I showed her the email and when she finished reading, she looked at me calmly and said "Si this man's just being honest with you and saying that the meditations you are doing are causing you more harm than good. He left his number - call him".

I did, and this man seemed different. There was an honesty about him that cut through. When I explained my problem, he already knew my predicament and had an answer. And it wasn't to distract myself with positive thinking or get lost in guided fantasy practices. He himself was aware of the dangers of those seemingly harmless feelgood exercises.

He straight up pointed out that my problem was suppressed resentment. That unrecognised it is left to stew and cause all sorts of emotional disturbances and symptoms. That just having knowledge of my character defects was not enough.

He told me that if I was willing to sit still a [ ] [ ]
thoughts using a unique Non-contemplati
exercise, to observe the resentment and fea. ...
cropped up through the light of consciousness, the problem
would lose its grip and flee. It sounded heady, but this man
was making sense to me. He explained why I could never
shake the feelings of restlessness under the surface no
matter how much I tried.

He told me that once anger was removed, all the symptoms
of the resentment energy I was suppressing such as the
depression, anxiety and feelings of discomfort I couldn't put
my finger on would leave without any effort on my part. That
I would reconnect to the God given intuitive consciousness
I was born with and begin to live with a metaphysical
defence against stress. No longer suffering it's damaging
mental and physical effects. I would no longer suffer from
obsessive behaviours and thinking, as there would be no
internal discomforts to seek relief from. I would live
objectively to my thoughts and negative emotions in the
present moment. That light would part me from darkness by
simply sitting still and allowing it to happen using the
meditation he offered.

It sounded too simple and something within me got angry at
the mere thought of its effectiveness. But I had nothing to
lose. I began the meditation with an attitude of 'Yeah

.atever'. A few days later I had an experience, not unlike the one I had in my flat a year before, and I knew then I had found the solution to my living problem. And through being freed from the anger I had accumulated over the year and returning to consciousness. I finally found a way to live that would not only change my path, but the paths of those around me. I began to understand what had happened to me. What happens to all of us on some level.

Resentment was my Fathers problem and most likely his Fathers problem. It is an invisible negative force working through emotions that runs through families - through generations. Transferred from parents to unsuspecting children sometimes by something as little as impatience, yet the damage can be as long affecting to that child as rage and anger would be. Reason being they have become affected by something they are unaware of, as was I. An ever-growing sense of separation and conflict of spirit and emotions took place within me as I struggled with the mental health problems and obsessive behaviours that manifested as a result of angers residency. Light and dark cannot exist in the same space, one I was born with, and the other exists only to create suffering and eventually took over the wheel of my life. Growing up I grew to believe that the cruelty in the world was normal, that the anger in me was normal as I adjusted to the discomfort I felt. *Anger/resentment was not a normal healthy emotion I had to somehow manage as I had been taught in therapy. It was a force I needed to be freed from.* And until that happened through a simple practice of sitting still and allowing light to enter and remove it, I would have continued to suffer. As I experienced throughout my life, forces of light and dark in this world are very real. And if It hadn't been for Stacey suggesting that I called a stranger who knew something I didn't, I would never have discovered the truth about my condition for myself. I would have never experienced real freedom and a new way of facing life. My pride would have destroyed all I had worked for.

*

Everything changed for me and my family in finding this unique meditation. I stopped struggling with my thoughts. I also stopped doubting and second guessing my decisions when we met a stressful event on the road. Life instantly opened-up with a new clarity. I discovered a way to practice love and patience without trying to willfully force those principles into my life. They just became a part of my existence through observing my thoughts from an awakened, neutral position and staying conscious and vigilant to negative emotions within myself. My mental health drastically improved. Relationships with others also improved as fears and anxieties fell away and I no longer needed to gain approval to feel validation. I felt complete in myself for the first time in my life. I had rediscovered the natural God given discernment and consciousness I was born with. I was no longer being driven by erratic emotions or dragged into others unbalanced emotional dramas. Now guided by intuition I became genuinely useful without any selfish motives behind my actions. I rediscovered a connection to the light we all have access to - if you know how it's done.

Life continued with its highs and lows and for the most I remained unaffected and was able meet each stressful event with a new awareness and perspective. Yet there was an event coming our way beyond anything I could have predicted. That would bring more stress and pressure on our family than I imagined could be possible. And it all began in the winter of 2016.

Chapter 7

The magic number!

Buying a new house is a stressful experience without a doubt. Dealing with solicitors, waiting on dates, packing up and relocating. We moved into our small three-bedroom home at the end of November 2016. The decision to get a three bed was based on the possibility and hope of a baby arriving at some point. My wife didn't seem to be dealing with the move so well. It should have been a time of excitement and new beginnings but instead it felt like the tension was being wound up on our marriage more than it had been for months.

It made the run up to Christmas difficult. We had dealt with a lot during our five years together. I had lost work due to injuries; my mum was diagnosed with cancer and Stacey was dealing with her own anxieties surrounding being in a relationship after losing Frankie's dad. All couples have their own trials to face and I felt we had dealt with all of ours well. We always emerged on the other side a little stronger. But by the time we moved home that winter, things were changing between us and it seemed that the main problem was down to the fears around our inability to conceive.

We had both decided a month before our wedding day, almost two years prior, that Stacey would stop using contraception and that we would try for a little brother or sister for Frankie. The whole process became one of disappointments and stress, especially for Stacey. It was a time in our relationship that brought frustration and arguments. Stacey has PCOS - polycystic ovary syndrome. It made the chances of her conceiving and carrying a child much lower. Although we did hold hope that she would eventually, after all, she had successfully brought Frankie into the world. But seven years had gone by since then, which was another factor not in our favor. Stacey was thirty-two and I was forty-one.

We thought for a while it may have been me that was failing to produce what was needed. A sperm test came back with positive results to my relief, but this only seemed to make things worse for Stacey. Three false positive pregnancy tests brought even more strain over those months. I remember well the feeling of elation at the thought that it was finally going to happen, only to discover it wasn't to be. By the last false positive test, it was easier to keep our efforts to ourselves. Breaking the news to others just filled us with more of a sense of failure. The clocks were ticking, and my wife especially had begun to lose hope.

We had spoken with a fertility specialist at the hospital a

month or so before the move. There were plans to begin down the route of fertility treatment in the February of the new year. We were concerned about that process because it brought its own set of problems and fears - one of them being the possibility of a multiple pregnancy - which neither of us were ready to deal with. But it would be a risk we would have to take.

Stacey's moods from the day we moved brought only tension. It got to the point that I was unable to talk to her about what she was feeling anymore. She had no interest in decorating our new home together or getting settled. If anything, it was clear that she felt uncomfortable in our new surroundings. I knew change was difficult for her, so as much as I put it down to that, the difficulty in our relationship had begun to reach an unavoidable climax. Neither of us were happy anymore. She was suffering, and it was difficult to watch. I had poured everything into making a good life for her and Frankie over the years, but I feared we were reaching a breaking point. I began to resent her attitude towards me, and although I could see it was all driven by her own conflicts, I was struggling to stay unaffected. For the first time in our relationship I began to experience doubts about our marriage. And as much as I tried to rationalise and excuse our problems as mere bumps in the road, I couldn't avoid them any longer. My wife was unhappy.

Christmas came around quick and brought what we both felt was a much-needed break staying with Stacey's family. It was obvious from the time we arrived that Stacey's intolerance was stretching further than me; she was short tempered with her whole family. It was not a relaxing time for either of us. Her whole attitude towards me was ice cold. At one point her two sisters and Mum point-blank told her to accept she was pregnant. They were met with let's say, a somewhat negative response. Then Stacey began to feel nauseous at certain smells.

She couldn't enjoy a drink, and certain foods made her want to vomit. She put her sensory intolerances down to the fact that she had caught the stomach bug her nephew was suffering from when we had arrived. Her Mum was convinced it was sickness caused by pregnancy. Stacey didn't want to even consider that possibility. Another false positive was too much to deal with for her by that point.

We left Stacey's parents more stressed than when we arrived. We headed home planning to see the New Year in at our house with my wife's parents travelling down to join us a couple of days later. About an hour into the journey Stacey had me stop at the nearest shop. She was desperate for a packet of ginger biscuits. As you may know, ginger is a natural settler for morning sickness. I was already aware of this as Stacey had told me how she used ginger when pregnant with Frankie to settle her feelings of sickness. It was the first moment that alerted me to the possibility her Mum was right, and that there was more to my wife's apparent problems than I thought.

We got home and the air of tension followed us in like an ever-looming black cloud. Stacey just got angrier and more agitated at the mention of a pregnancy test. The day before her parents turned up, she began shouting at me in the kitchen about something minor. And just before I stomped out to go shopping and cool off, she said she had no interest in sorting anything out with me. I stated that things between us needed to change and she told me that she didn't care what I thought. I left feeling like we had finally reached the point of no return. Communication seemed to have deteriorated to nothing.

I called after I left to say that after her parents had gone, we would have to decide the best arrangements for all of us. In my head I felt we were over. I called a friend to air my frustration and sadness, I explained to him that I couldn't stay with someone who was so unhappy with me. I knew I loved her, but I knew for her wellbeing that I would have let her go. I also needed to consider my own mental health. I was at a loss for what else to do.

My mother-in-law Di is a no-nonsense woman, and she was not accepting that Stacey's moods and sickness were down to anything but a pregnancy. When she arrived at our house, she managed to convince Stacey to at least buy a home test. Yet there was still a definite wall of denial up between my wife and the thought of her being pregnant. That was the day before our second wedding anniversary. The following morning, we both lay in bed and talked about her reluctance to take the test. She was full of fear that it would be another false positive. That fear had been the real source of all her agitation.

I admitted I was also feeling the pressure that we may not be able to conceive naturally. For the first time in a while we spoke honestly and openly with each other about how we were both feeling. In the end I managed to convince her to take the test on the premise that at least we would know one way or the other, and it was best to know where we stood than spend any-more time reacting to the agitations and fears of what might be. If the test was negative, we would accept it and move on. She went to the bathroom, and I took a deep breath and braced myself for more disappointment.

After what seemed like ages she finally emerged with a wide grin on her face and holding a test showing two prominent lines. My wife was pregnant! I was to become a biological Father. We held each other tight and both shed a few tears of relief. I was overwhelmed with excitement. Her parents also felt the alleviation of stress around our situation. This wasn't a mistake. It explained her moods and sickness over the previous weeks. It was also a good feeling to know that my wife didn't just hate me. She was carrying our baby.

I headed to the supermarket that morning for supplies. My heart was racing at the news. It was a pivotal moment of my existence and one that happened at exactly the right moment in my life. I kept getting flashback memories of darker places I had been during the drive. In the past the thought of becoming a parent terrified me, but when I found out that morning that we were expecting I felt nothing but gratitude for where I was in life. As I walked around the supermarket, chest puffed out with a big smile on my face I suddenly got hit with deep emotion that came from no-where. I burst into tears in the middle of the milk aisle. And not just a few tears, I was sobbing my heart out. I felt like the most blessed man on earth. I will never forget our second wedding anniversary; it was a wonderful day. Don't get me wrong, my wife was still agitated, struggling with her moods and treating me like I was the most annoying man on the planet, but less so now she understood why. She kept saying that this pregnancy felt so much different to when she carried Frankie, but we put that down to her age and health. She was already beginning to show a little bump, so a dating scan was booked for the following week. We worked out by the bump and the way she felt emotionally that she was probably around three months gone.

All the concern and worry about our marriage dissolved in the milk aisle. Yes, my wife was still cranky with me, but for a very good reason. What she was suffering emotionally was for us as a family. The week that led up to the scan was a relaxing time. We saw the new year in with Stacey's parents and my Mum and Auntie. My Mum had survived and fully recovered from cancer the previous year to look forward to becoming a Nanny for the first time and she was so excited for us. As was my Auntie who had been incredibly supportive of me over the years as I got sober and began to piece my life back together. She was a social worker and loved nothing more than to see someone who had struggled begin to succeed in life. I returned to my job as a welder the week after the Christmas and new-year break with a bounce in my step and a real sense of purpose. Life was looking good for us.

Frankie was also excited but also carrying her own little worries and concerns around the arrival of a new sibling. A new baby would be as big a deal for Frankie as it was for my wife and me. A couple of days before the scan, Frankie, after being up in bed for an hour came back down and stood in the living-room doorway, clutching her go-to dolly with red cheeks and tears rolling down her face. I walked over, picked her up and took her into the kitchen, sat her on the worktop and asked her what was wrong. She sadly asked "Daddy, Mummy's not going to have twins is she"? Frankie picks up most conversations us grown up's have as little ears often do. She had overheard us talking about the possibility of having twins because of fertility treatment. You see Frankie had, over time, come around to the idea of perhaps having a little sister, she wasn't too fussed on a boisterous brother but even if that be the case, she was now ready to share Mum and me with a baby. Only the one though! No-more than that. And it was understandable, Frankie had lived with the spotlight on her for the whole nine years of her life, and the idea of two siblings running riot was not a thought she was willing to entertain.

So, I reassured her "No Honey that would have only been a possibility had we had fertility treatment. But Mummy and I didn't need to start down that road. I promise it will be just the one and no more". I must admit we were all a little relieved that possibility had been removed from the equation. I mean, I was a first-time parent embarking on the baby journey from the start, one was plenty enough for me and my wife.

The Friday morning came around quick. I left work and got home to an excited wife. I was absolutely buzzing that we would see our child for the first time and hear their heartbeat. We arrived at the local hospital for the dating scan and checked in at the desk. I couldn't sit still with excitement, which was really irritating my wife, but I couldn't help it. Eventually we were called into the scan room. Stacey lay back on the bed and was prepared for the examination. The gel was applied to her belly, and the Sonographer went to work. My wife asked just after she had begun "Is there a heartbeat?" The sonographer replied "Yes, I've found the heartbeat". She continued to look for what seemed like ages, moving the camera, tapping buttons, moving the camera some more, until she came to a stop, removed the camera from Stacey's bump and asked us "Are you ready for this"? I immediately began to worry that perhaps something was wrong.

She looked at us smiling and held up three fingers. Stacey looked at me grinning and we both laughed at the accuracy of our guess of twelve weeks, as in 'three months'. It was after all the dating scan. She immediately corrected us, "No, there are three heartbeats. Congratulations, you are having triplets"!

There are moments of shock and disbelief that can happen to us throughout life that almost cause time to stop. This was one of those moments. As my heart sped up and my whole body got charged with an energy like nothing I had physically experienced before, I burst out into loud uncontrollable laughter. I couldn't stop. The sonographer had replaced the camera on my wife's belly and was pointing at the TV screen which I was staring at, wide eyed and belly laughing. It was clear to see. Three little dots, three little heartbeats, three little growing lives. We had somehow been blessed with triplets after being told our chances of conceiving were low. We had been due to start fertility treatment the following month! I felt I was experiencing a miracle, a gift – three gifts!

In my shock, I had almost forgotten that my wife was there. When I turned from the screen to look at her, what I saw was a response that was the exact opposite of mine. She was shaking and in her eyes was fear. I had never seen my wife look that way before. She refused to believe it. "Look again, that's not fucking right, it can't be right! I can't have triplets!" She was clearly distressed, she demanded at least three more checks, but there was no mistake, they were there. Eventually the Sonographer called in a colleague for a second opinion on my wife's request. I was still laughing uncontrollably in shock myself, but I was quickly beginning to feel concerned for my wife - her shock wasn't passing. I was holding her hand and trying to comfort her, but she was traumatized. It was a bizarre situation to be in. Me laughing with tears of joy, my wife shaking and crying with fear. Once the sonographer had finished scanning, Stacey immediately made a brief phone call to her mum, crying and telling her the news. Her mum was in total shock, as were we.

It felt as though were out of the little scan room as fast as we were taken in. My heart was still racing, my wife still shaking as we were ushered into a side office and met by two midwives. They sat us down and it was explained we had a set of twins and a singleton. The technical term for our set up was 'Dichorionic Triamniotic triplets', so 'mono' twins sharing a single placenta plus a single foetus doing their own thing. The chances of it happening naturally were in the tens of thousands to one. We were also informed that it was a very high-risk pregnancy, so Stacey and the babies would be monitored closely with fortnightly scans. We would also have a specialist dealing with us.

We were told that there was also the option to reduce, which meant the termination of one or two of our growing babies. That last piece of information really took me by shock, Stacey also said it was out of the question although it wasn't how my wife was really feeling. The entire last half hour of my life had felt completely surreal.

The meeting was over as quickly as that. We were given the date for the next scan. They told my wife there was a local group for mothers of multiples she may like to contact. When I asked if there was anyone I could speak to, perhaps a group of some sort for some advice or experience. My enquiry was met with an apology, there was nothing. I was on my own with a panicked wife carrying three babies facing a high-risk pregnancy and no idea what was ahead of me.

We left in total shock. Stacey was seven weeks and three days pregnant.

Chapter 8

Aftershock

My first phone call on leaving the hospital was to my mum while Stacey called her sisters who didn't believe the news. It took Stacey a while to convince them it was true, and she wasn't winding them up for a laugh. My shock announcement to mum was met with a long pause, followed by an awkward laughter and a half-concerned, half disbelieving "No way"! She was as genuinely as stunned as we were. My mum has no other grandchildren other than Frankie, who she treats as her own. To be told, after being given the all clear from cancer that previous year, that she was looking at becoming a Nanny to triplets was information that took some processing. Stacey's mum was equally as taken back. To the mums this was a miracle in their lifetimes.

I have a good friend who has been an ear on the end of the phone through some difficult times. He introduced me to the meditation and has become my most trusted friend, one who talks with a no-nonsense honesty and straightforwardness that many might struggle to get past. He was my next phone call. His response was not unlike mine had been in the Sonography room.

"Paddy, you'll never guess what mate......It's Triplets".

My shock announcement was met with belly laughter, many congratulations and a few expletives. I was pacing around the car park, talking at speed and excitedly going over the last hour's events. My wife had returned to the car by that point and was just sat in shock. As I talked on the phone, I looked up to my wife. I was still high with adrenalin but her face I will never forget. She was frightened. There was no sense of joy, or acceptance of the situation for her. I honestly thought that her initial shock and fear would have subsided after a moments processing, but it was quickly becoming apparent that we were in two very different places with our news. There was a naive part of me that couldn't really understand my wife's initial response. Why wasn't she as happy as I was? Here we are, struggling to conceive, and we have been blessed with a lottery win multiple pregnancy. My concern for her was growing as we left the hospital.

The easiest way to explain the feeling of discovering we were having triplets that morning would be to imagine yourself switching on the radio to hear announcements that extra-terrestrial beings had landed on earth. And that we had welcomed them, and our planet and population would be moving to a parallel dimension next week for our own interests, so cancel your TV subscription and only pack what you really need. It all sounds highly unlikely and extremely

89

far-fetched. But the news we had just taken in was just as surreal a situation.

We left the hospital and drove to my wife's workplace so Stacey could discuss with her boss her work plans for the coming months now she was pregnant. Stacey was quiet for most of the journey. I kept being hit with the same conscious thought (amongst the many others racing through my head), that this would not have happened if my wife and I didn't have what it took to pull it off. I felt amazing, on top of the world. I was still on a high from the positive pregnancy test the week before, just from knowing I was to become a father to one baby. But to discover we had three took my elation to a whole new level. I wasn't fully aware of - or wasn't even considering in fact - the risks that we were facing in all my excitement. And that was the difference between my reaction and my wife's that morning. It was all well and good, me through the roof with excitement but it was my wife who would have to safely carry them. And as we were soon to discover, the risks were endless.

Stacey's Boss and work colleagues were in as much disbelief as everyone else was. It was agreed that she would continue to work until she was unable to do her job (or get in and out of the car on her own). As a care worker in the community her job involves a lot of lifting. It was clear from the size of the bump at seven weeks that it was going to become challenging for her to carry out her daily duties at work much sooner rather than later.

We left her workplace and went for something to eat. There were moments we would both be laughing in between the moments of realisation. It wasn't long before the conversation turned to Frankie whom we were collecting from school later that afternoon. Only a couple of days prior I had reassured her she would only be having the one sibling, now we had to break it to her she would have three! We were both dreading telling her and we began rehearsing how we would put it to her, but there was no way of making light of it. It felt like we both had a shameful confession to cough up to her. As my wife said, "this is going to break her heart". Alongside my wife's fear and concern that day I did my best to take stock and keep it positive somehow. It wasn't easy.

Stacey walked round to the school yard while I waited in the car out front. My brother-in-law spotted me as he arrived to collect his boys from the school, he had obviously heard the news judging by his laughter and comments about my impressive manly abilities. Shortly after I spotted Stacey and a sobbing Frankie walk through the gate towards the car. Stacey had already broken the news to her, and she didn't take it well at all. In fact, she hardly spoke, her spirit was as low as her Mum's. When we arrived home, Stacey went to our bedroom and stayed there for the rest of the weekend.

I had a gig locally with my band that night. Stacey was happy for me to go so I took the opportunity to go and burn off some energy. It also gave my wife some time to talk with Frankie and chat with her Mum and sisters about that day's events. My hope was that they would calm her enough to see some clarity around what was happening with us. I got a phone call later that evening, it was my wife to explain that if she was to reduce the pregnancy, she would need my support. It was news that shocked me. I already felt it inappropriate that the midwives had even given us that option in the emotionally charged state we were in. It didn't sit right with me at all in the light of our remarkable situation.

She was already feeling pressure from me simply because I was so excited. I knew we needed time to talk it out, but I also had to consider that a final decision to reduce the pregnancy would ultimately come down to her. I told her that I would support her if that was what she needed to do, and that I didn't want her to feel any pressure from me. But I also knew that I didn't want her to make any rash decisions. We needed to know and fully understand the risks. If it came down to terminating one or two of the triplets for whatever reason it would have to be a conscious decision made with clarity and with a full understanding of the danger's we were facing. Fear only clouds judgment. Deep down, it was a decision I never really wanted to have to consider, all I saw was a miracle.

It was an emotionally hard weekend for all of us for different reasons. Stacey never left our bedroom. She cried, got angry and upset at the slightest mention of possibly carrying all three babies. She also asked me not to refer to them as the triplets because she didn't want me getting attached to them, I found that difficult to hear from her. We had also done some research into the risks involved in her carrying the three babies. And the risks were as big to Stacey's health and life as they were to the triplets. This only fanned the flames of fear that had gripped her and in short, made matters worse. Unfortunately, they were risks we had to be aware of.

On the Monday morning whilst at work, I received a call from my wife. She was clearly distressed. Stacey had made the decision that a reduction was the only safe option for her health and the chances of any of the remaining babies' survival. She was adamant it needed to be done and that I needed to leave work, pick her up and take her to the hospital to discuss her decision and get the ball rolling. I left for home to meet Stacey. I felt awful that my wife was suffering so much and there was nothing I could say that would change her mind to give all three babies a chance.

We headed straight over to our local hospital. Stacey had a sense of relief about her, the more she spoke about it being the right thing to do on the drive over, the more it just sounded like she was just trying to convince herself. I was struggling so much with my conscience at that point. To have been blessed with these three gifts of life, only to terminate one or two of them for no other reason than fear without even speaking with a specialist and fully understanding our situation was making me feel extremely uncomfortable.

We spoke with the receptionist and explained the situation. My wife asked to speak directly with the midwife who had seen us after the scan on the Friday before - the one who had mentioned reduction as an option. We were asked to wait in a side room while the midwife was located. Ten silent minutes went by before the receptionist returned. The midwife that Stacey needed to speak to was not in that day. Neither was our specialist who would be assigned to us for the duration of the pregnancy. We were informed that there was no-one who could help us with that enquiry that morning. And so, we left. My wife overwhelmed with fear again and in tears. And me, quietly thanking God with everything I had for some more time and an opportunity to hopefully help my wife to see past some of her fear.

It was in that moment I knew exactly what my job was to be. As I left that hospital it was clear that emotionally I needed to remain as solid for my wife and Frankie as I would have to have been for one baby. If I wanted to have a chance at us keeping the triplets, I knew there were no words I could produce that were going to change her mind about the fears she felt. And it wasn't just the risks of the pregnancy that were causing those fears. She was terrified I would not be able to cope with her and three babies and would walk out the door, leaving her alone to deal with them. I had never had experience with babies before, let alone three at the same time. She was aware of the changes and pressures one baby can bring to a relationship. There were fears that what she would go through physically and emotionally that might cause her to miscarry one or all of them. She knew full well my past and my previous failings at dealing with life and my history of walking when things got too much. Even though I had not let her down, it was going to be a show of my consistency, involvement, courage and strengths that would be the only things that would convince her I had what it took to be what she needed if we were to go ahead with the triplets. I could not fail her - neither could I fail them or Frankie. My real purpose as an expectant father and a husband was handed to me that day.

Chapter 9

Finding my role

In recovering from many of my own mental health conflicts I had a clear understanding of fear and resentment, and how those forces can directly affect an individual and family unit. When I left home, I left a stressed environment. My father's mental health had deteriorated to breaking point as his chronic morphine addiction and drinking slowly ate away at his sanity. None of us escaped that home unscathed.

The resentments he harboured towards his own Father and his failings to meet his expectations in life in turn became my resentments. His anger became mine. As the saying goes 'the apple doesn't fall too far from the tree'. It is a dark lineage of resentment energy that runs in families, passing down from generation to generation through impatience and intolerance. An inability and unwillingness to forgive our tormentors allows it to continue. I don't believe any of the mental health problems I developed, or my alcoholism came down to any genetic bullets. It is my opinion that the depression, anxiety and paranoia, all the obsessive self-damaging behaviours as well as the more serious diagnoses I was treated for in the past were just symptoms of the anger that I had buried. They were created by the pressure and conflicts of my frustration and bitterness at life. I was a boiling pot, in a constant battle with myself to keep the lid sealed.

As a recovered alcoholic and addict I have since worked with many men and women whose own paths of destructive behaviours can all be traced back to a single cause. Unrecognised and suppressed resentment passed on to them unknowingly through their parent's own inability to deal with stress. It was with this knowledge taken from experience that I went into my relationship with Stacey. If my family was to thrive, it was my job as Dad to place love and tolerance at the centre of my life. The spirit of resentment that had passed down through my family had to stop with me. In order to be a father who would have a chance at raising a healthy family I needed to approach that role differently than the men in my family had done before me. My wife had miscarried twice before Frankie, both times in a highly stressful relationship and she is convinced the stress caused her losses. I saw my responsibility in that pregnancy with a sharp clarity. I had to simply stay out of anger and keep my cool.

*

I had never seen my wife in such despair as I did at that time. In what should have been a period of celebration, instead she swiftly sank into a deep depression in the weeks following our scan. Our home returned to being one full of tension. It would have been too easy for me to react and retaliate to her cutting remarks and mood swings. But I saw her fear for what it was, and I didn't resent her for the way she felt. It became my priority to stay aware of my own fears and beware of the temptation to get lost in them. The meditation I practice kept me in a neutral place where observing thoughts, good and bad, without reacting was possible. Neither Stacey nor Frankie needed me disappearing into darkness up my own backside. It wasn't an easy task; the worries cropping up in my head became almost overwhelming at times.

For a start I had financial concerns. The house would now be too small, I would need a bigger car and how was I going to afford all the equipment we would need for three babies with one wage coming in? My wife was going to have to quit work and we would surely feel the sting of that. The list was never ending and the rising temptation to worry was relentless. But looking back – that impending mountain climb was not so tough. We managed quite easily to financially adjust and get what was needed for the house a little bit at a time. We were also blessed to have family help us out with bits and pieces we would need.

The most important thing for me as the man of a very tense

house, was to stay in the present and remain conscious. To keep my wife calm and not burden her with my worries for her wellbeing and those of the triplets and of course, to keep Frankie fully involved and feeling loved. Each day I got up and got on with it. I worked hard and did my best to keep a level head. The meditation exercise and the awareness it gave me brought defence against the constant rising fear in me. My family were all facing the unknown. I lived through it one day at a time without any expectations.

That first week, between my wife's family phoning with upbeat messages and support and my own strategically placed input, we managed to tentatively persuade Stacey to hold back from rushing to reduce. Even if only temporarily it was a positive move towards going ahead with the pregnancy. It caused numerous arguments between us though, and I kept watchful of the resentment she had growing towards me for wanting to give them a chance. I wasn't blind to the reluctance to carry them that my wife was living with, I just bit my tongue because I couldn't ignore the intuitive sense of purpose I felt around the whole event. Every fibre in me believed it was supposed to happen - to somehow benefit all of us.

It was my first time living with a pregnant woman. And without practicing tolerance and leaving my pride at the door each day I would have had no chance of coping. I don't believe there is any preparation that can put a partner in total understanding, or at a completely safe range from the incoming firestorm of a woman during a multiple pregnancy. When we found out a baby was on the way (just the one that is) I ordered a book about pregnancy, to give me an idea of what may be ahead. It also gave my wife a little confidence in my show of interest. It was a good read. It explained the three trimesters/stages of pregnancy. What a woman goes through and what to expect. On the discovery of multiples, the book I ordered meant little. I understood that I was in for a rough ride, and maybe I was naive in my positive approach to it all (I really did have no idea what was ahead). The changes Stacey would go through would be extreme. She would need my support and care from day one. This was no normal pregnancy in any sense. I would have to step up and take over much of the daily duties at home. It wasn't just the physical strain that would burden her as the weeks passed, it was the enormous emotional changes she was dealing with that would need my upmost patience. I didn't fully know it then, but we were facing the ultimate test of our marriage.

We searched for as much information on the pregnancy as possible before the next scan which came around in the blink of an eye. We live in small town which has a district hospital with a women's unit and maternity ward in which my wife and stepdaughter were both born. It was only fitting that if the triplets were to make it, they would join the world in the same unit. In the days leading up to the scan my wife began what would be the start of a good few hunches that she had lost one of them.

"You need to be prepared for that Si, it's a big possibility" she would warn me.

I felt like she was trying to knock me down a little with her remarks and I also got the feeling she was hoping it would be true. It would mean a natural reduction, one in which the decision was made for us. It would eliminate any guilt that we would have undoubtedly struggled with if we were going to terminate. Fortnightly scans are typical with a high-risk pregnancy as there is much that can go wrong. It is imperative to the health of Mum and babies that a close eye is kept on developments. We had mono twins and a singleton. Mono twins share a placenta and so the main risk to them was twin to twin transfusion. It happens when the stronger of the two babies takes more nutrients from the placenta. When this occurs, it can literally kill off the weaker baby, or at best leave one twin underdeveloped with permanent lifelong conditions and complications. It can also result in the death of the larger twin – a lose/lose situation.

We checked in at the desk and waited to be called. We were also meeting with our specialist consultant after the scan who we understood would be seeing us through the pregnancy. At each of the scans, the sonographer always began the same way. They went straight for the heartbeats. I always felt apprehension before the examinations, as did my wife but for other reasons. The sonographer placed the camera on Stacey's ever-growing bump and moved it around. With a smile she excitedly declared "There they all are! - three strong heartbeats". I exhaled with relief. My wife's hunch was wrong.

Our specialist consultant was a kind man with a relaxed demeanour. He put Stacey's mind at ease and she instantly liked him for it. At that meeting we talked about possible arrival dates. It had to be an elected date as no hospital wants to deal with an emergency triplet birth. Everything concerning the arrival needed to be pre-planned and organised. Had it been a normal pregnancy the full-term arrival date would have been the 19th of August, but it's different with multiples. In the U.K triplets are never usually left to bake past 34 weeks. The main reason being they don't want to risk an emergency labour. The other obvious factor was that my wife was carrying three babies. She would eventually be on bed rest with the weight and pressure of the size of the bump she would develop. My wife is a petite lady, she was going to go through the mill with this pregnancy.

We were also told a decision had been made with our local

hospital that the fortnightly scans would be alternated between themselves and a bigger city hospital. Stacey wasn't overly impressed as it meant travel which would eventually become uncomfortable, but it was a sound decision. The city hospital had a unit that dealt specifically with high risk multiples. They had better scan equipment that would greatly improve chances of discovering any problems on the way.

That meeting brought a little relief, especially for Stacey. She was still struggling with the thought of carrying three babies, but we had a bit of a plan now and she was comfortable with the specialist at the local hospital. At least that was something positive. And I quietly let it sink in that all three were still in there, with strong heartbeats. It just reinforced the feeling I had that our situation was supposed to be. We just needed to get through the next two weeks until the next scan without any medical issues.

My excitement continued to grate on my wife. I tried hard to contain it, but it wasn't easy. I don't think I've ever come down from that surge I felt at the dating scan. For weeks all I could say was 'Triplets' out loud and in my head like it was some newly discovered word full of weight and depth that had been brought into existence just for me. I was walking the dog one morning and bumped into my neighbours (who I had never had conversation with) and just blurted out that

I was having triplets. They looked positively puzzled and a bit confused as I laughed and walked off. I would find myself giggling to myself at the thought of what was occurring in my life. I would be at work welding under a car, focused on my job then suddenly remember that we had somehow conceived triplets and start laughing out loud. It was surreal, and it still feels that way.

I can't describe this without it coming across as a little crazy, which was certainly the way my wife saw it, but I felt a connection to those three growing lives from the day we discovered them. I was bonded to them from day one. I never once doubted them. I called my best friend on one occasion early in the pregnancy and explained to him that even with all the risks, I intuitively knew they were going to be okay. It bothered my wife because she had been through two miscarriages and had, through some-kind of emotional defence mechanism learned to disconnect from the baby she was carrying. She had done it with Frankie, and it was only when Frankie was born safely that she bonded with her. I knew she was worried about me, not so much my seemingly naive attitude but more how I would deal with losing one, two - or all of them. The way I saw it, if nature was going to take its course it was out of my hands. That would be easier to deal with rather than us making that decision. It was my faith in the triplets as gifts of grace that kept me out of a lot of fears. It also kept me unwavering and hopeful when my wife would get overwhelmed. We left the hospital and life carried on. It didn't feel normal by any measure, but we did our best to get through the days as a family.

I took a small loan out in those early weeks which solved a few financial concerns, and I busied myself with a garden project which came as a welcomed distraction while we waited for the big city scan. When we bought the house, the garden was just a flat square of mud. It was getting me down looking at it, so it was a good opportunity to get a job done for the coming spring/summer months. I wanted Frankie to have a nice garden to play in, and maybe one day for the triplets to enjoy too. It kept me occupied while we edged our way towards the next examination. This was a scan that came with a warning from our little hospital. We had a very high-risk pregnancy which involved a world of possible outcomes. We were told that we had to be prepared to sit through a talk about those risks at the city scan, that they would not hold back on the punches and that they would lay it on thick. We both felt we had informed ourselves enough on our pregnancy by that point to be aware of most of the risks though - surely nothing could bring any more shock to us in our current situation.

CHAPTER 10

CRASHING BACK TO EARTH

The drive to the city for the next scan took about an hour and forty-five minutes. I came to enjoy those drives as they allowed a precious opportunity for my wife and I to regroup away from the distractions of home and work. We were able to talk openly and take stock of our situation.

By the time the city scan came around it seemed my wife had found a spark of acceptance regarding her pregnancy. She was by no means comfortable with the idea of triplets yet, but she had begun processing it and working out the practicalities of how we would manage. To me it brought hope and seemed a step in the right direction. Frankie had also gradually found her own sense of acceptance with it - so long as they were all girls!

The hospital we attended was St Michaels in Bristol. The unit we were seen in specialised in multiple and high-risk pregnancies. We were lucky to have such a specialised unit so close to where we lived. Bristol is also a city I know well. It is where my family on my Mother's side are from, and still live.

I knew the steep streets surrounding the hospital from walking them as a little kid, though I hadn't been to that area for a few decades. My Italian Grandmother, Maria, lived in a block of flats in the Stokes Croft area near the hospital. She lived on the twelfth floor and I remember standing on the balcony when we would visit, looking out over the city. It seemed immense as a child.

We had always lived in the sticks, far from anyone or anything. So, to be in such a stimulating environment was mind blowing. I loved everything about that city. The seedy -dank underpasses with the bad buskers, the vibrant colours and having my eyes opened to the different aspects of a vast multicultural world. The old buildings, the waterfront with the boats and ships, bars full of life and hustle & bustle. Hot city nights soaking in the muffled sounds below; the near and far wails of sirens, heavy with unseen drama and chaos across the far-reaching orange glow I gazed across with excitement from the bedroom window up in our tower, firing my overactive imagination. It had a pulse and a humming danger that somehow appealed and excited something in me.

Those memories came flooding back as we walked into the waiting room on that bright sunny Friday morning, where I was met with the nostalgic view of my Nan's block of flats across the tops of the houses, buildings and tree line. It was hard to believe where my life had taken me since childhood. To have been where I had been in the world and made it to that point. It made me smile to think I was back, looking out at the same view decades later but now with a wife pregnant with triplets and a stepdaughter who called me Daddy. I was finally at a stable place in my life, mentally and emotionally. Maria would have been overjoyed to know there were triplets coming. Family and grandchildren meant everything to her as she grew older. She would have been so proud - and everyone back in Naples would have known all about it.

Occasionally in life I have come across people who give off an unshakable natural confidence carried by a searing honesty. Our specialist Dr Dean was one of those people. He called us through the heavy double doors through to the ward, into a side room and then left. I recognised the scan equipment, there looked to be more of it in this hospital which could only be a good thing. The Sonographer got Stacey comfortable on the bed for the examination. She was quick to find three heartbeats. Stacey said we had yet to hear them and the sonographer positioned the camera, hit a button on the console and boom! There it was, that first pounding heartbeat and we got to hear all three. They sounded strong.

It was another pivotal moment of my life. Those three

heartbeats made everything seem even more real. The scan went without any problems and the sonographer was happy and asked us to wait in the room as Dr Dean would be coming back through to talk to us. Frankie was taken through to a side room to talk with a nurse as the conversation that was coming was not for her young ears.

Dr Dean walked in, sat down in front of us and quietly looked down at our notes, flicking through the pages as we waited with anticipation. He asked me directly what we had – what was the type of triplet pregnancy? I told him with confidence and a smile 'Spontaneous Dichorionic Triamniotic triplets, the mono twins separated with a membrane'. He didn't smile and say well done which instantly pissed me off, he simply looked back down with a serious expression and flicked through our notes again. He eventually placed the notes on the side desk, turned back to my wife and asked us if we were aware the risks involved with our type of pregnancy.

What came next was a barrage of negative outcomes and potential dangers. It was intense. The twins on their own were high risk because they shared a placenta. There was a big danger of twin to twin transfusion which we were already aware of. What made our pregnancy particularly dangerous was that we also had a singleton in there with its own placenta and amniotic sac. Any problems to the twins could not just pose a threat to the singleton but also to my wife. She was looking at big risks herself. From blood infections, as well as the obvious physical traumas she would endure as her body grew to accommodate the triplets. As for the triplets themselves it seemed that an outcome of all three surviving, or even making it to be healthy babies was slim. He explained that one or all of them could be born handicapped in some way. If they did survive, the twins could suffer from underdeveloped brains as they fought to share nutrients.

We could be facing a lifetime of taking care of permanently mentally and physically debilitated children. There was also the emotional impact it would have on us as a couple to consider. At one point I jumped in "But at least for now everything is good". He looked me dead in the eye and shot me down in four words, "That means absolutely nothing!" And he was right, optimism is a good thing, but the truth will always be the truth. Our situation could change from day to day, problems could develop at any stage. He brought us both crashing back down to earth, me particularly. A part of me felt anxious around the fact that I had been encouraging my wife to go through with such a risky pregnancy.

As we sat there my heart began sinking. It was a brutal talk, one that we both had to hear. Once he had explained the risks, we were given the safest option. It was tough listening. He said with no messing about,

"The safest option would be to reduce the twins. This would give the singleton a normal chance of developing. Leaving the twins to develop and reducing the singleton would still be high risk. There is also an option of surgery to remove just one of the twins so to give two babies chance. If you decide to do this - call me on Monday morning and let me know. I can get you in a London hospital next week and perform the procedure myself ".

Reality was flooring me. I was knocked off my feet for the first time by the true gravity of our situation and the dangers involved. When he was done, he asked us what we wanted to do. Deflated I looked at Stacey; she looked at the Dr and said, "We are going to give them all a chance". I was so surprised. The Dr smiled, clapped his hands and said "Good, then I will do everything I can to get them here safely", Before he left, he shook my hand firmly and advised me "look after her".

The three of us left the hospital, I was without any excitement this time, or funny comments to cheer my wife or Frankie up. It was a claustrophobic drive home. By the time we got back my wife was asking that we consider reducing again. It escalated into an argument. We were both feeling the fear and pressure of what may be ahead. I was trying to defend my feeling that they were gifts to us that I already felt a bond with. My argument felt loose in the light of the information we had just received at the hospital. It just fuelled Stacey's frustration. The way she saw it - I couldn't possibly have a bond with them.

My wife was upset again, as was Frankie. Stacey went to the bedroom and stayed there all weekend. It felt like we had taken a leap back to the first scan, except this time I was without the confidence and excitement to offer any hope to her. I had nothing to console her with. She later told me that in a way she was glad that the meeting with the Dr had hit me so hard, because it gave me an understanding of what she felt the whole time she was pregnant. For a moment we were on the same page, and it was not an enjoyable one. But it was one that if we had both stayed on would probably have destroyed our relationship and any chance of the triplets making it.

When fear takes a hold at the centre of a relationship, it eats away at anything worthwhile. I was hit hard with the facts, but even then, the intuitive sense that all would be well continued to rise above any fear I was experiencing. I know to my wife I came across as foolish for believing we had been blessed with these triplets, but I could not let any fears or doubts take the wheel. I had to brush myself off, not dwell on the hospital visit and get on with taking care of those under my roof. As I have said before, I knew a show of my confidence and emotional consistency would do more than any words to give my wife confidence in me. It may come across as male bravado, but I needed to push on for the sake of them. There would be time further down the line to discuss with her my own fears and concerns, there would be a time and a place. But this wasn't it. Sometimes to get up, dust off and push on is the only option.

It was the doctor's job to inform us of all the facts and possible outcomes. Part of me was angry at the bastard for putting us emotionally back a step but there was a more conscious part of me that appreciated his forwardness with us. Ever since getting sober I have a respect for people who forego any flattery or sugar coating in favour of delivering truth for someone's benefit, no matter how hard that truth may be to hear. These are people with whom you know exactly where you stand. My closest friends are such people, and in a hard situation they are the only friends to have.

There were three people with whom I spoke regularly during the pregnancy other than my mum. One of them a good friend who has a knack for keeping all things in a clear perspective and not allowing me to veer off into problems that haven't occurred yet. The other, a female friend who had been through two pregnancies herself and was able to give me some insight and perspective as to what a pregnant woman can go through emotionally. I was grateful for this insight as it was difficult to approach my wife to discuss any thoughts or concern's I had in respect to what she was going through, especially in the early stages of the pregnancy. The third 'phone a friend' was my Aunt Liz. She was the sort of person who had the natural ability to bring calm to any storm. She worked for years as a social worker, then later as a university lecturer and teacher in the same field. The last time I was at my Nan's in that block of flats in Bristol my father had come back drunk from an afternoon out drinking in the city, threatening suicide. My Nan called my Aunt Liz who dropped everything to drive over, and the minute I knew she was coming I felt safe - she had that sort of presence.

I didn't see her - or much of my family - for years after I left home and wandered into the world with my own developing problems. It was only when my mum got diagnosed with an aggressive Cancer, decades later that I really got to know Liz again. We wouldn't have coped with all that needed to be done whilst my mum was in hospital for treatment had it not been for Liz, she was a rock. When by some miracle my mother made a full recovery, Liz and I stayed in contact and we saw her regularly from that period in our lives. She always took an interest in what I was doing to improve my life and that of my family. She was over the moon when we bought the house, and again when I told her about the triplets. She brought it all straight back to the ground with sound advice for me as a man facing a pregnancy for the first time. There was nothing she loved more than to see someone succeed in life. Family to her meant everything, it was something she helped me see the importance of. She loved Stacey and Frankie as her own. To everyone she met she became Auntie Liz, no one was treated any differently by her – she had that effect on people.

In the second trimester of the pregnancy Liz was taken into hospital with hip pain. By the time they had discovered the cancer it had spread to her spine - too much to successfully treat. She died four weeks later, and we never got to say goodbye. It left all who knew her in total shock. No-one had a clue how ill she was. It hit me hard and was another emotional punch I had to keep from knocking me down. A bright light in our lives had gone out. But life had to continue – I had no choice but to carry on. It was months before I would even begin to process losing her.

We have a little Dog called Milo, I walked him a lot during the pregnancy and it was my opportunity to make those calls to my friends and my Aunt away from the tension of the house. I am forever grateful to those three voices on the end of the phone that didn't allow me to get swallowed up by fear and doubt. They all simply pointed me to the place I needed to remain - in the present moment. The only place my family would ever need me to be. And where I remain to this day.

Chapter 11

The weight

The days rolled on without any physical complications to Stacey or the babies. As expected, some of those days ran smoother than others. My wife got uncomfortable quickly with the growth of the triplets and it wasn't long before she had to give up her job. She gradually seemed to be coming around to the idea of becoming a triplet Mum. But the environment at home remained tense.

I had heard of post-natal depression in women, my wife however was suffering pre-natal depression during the pregnancy. It took me a while at times to step back from the frustration of not being able to get through to her, or to get her to open-up to me about what she was going through. I suffered depression for years and I know what it is to become so insular and disconnected from the world and the people in it. For the first time in my life I was the one dealing with someone suffering rather than the other way around.

Sometimes her remarks and swipes at me were so personal it was hard to not get pulled into arguments and retaliate in kind. But I knew from my own experience that what she was dealing with were the direct effects of fear and resentment.

117

She was scared that I would leave her, it was one of her biggest fears. I later found out she had a mass of worries concerning me and my ability to be able to cope with triplets. Much of her anger towards me was her reacting to imagined outcomes in which I let her down. Fear of the future is just anger refocused. She was getting pissed off with me for things I hadn't done – or may never do. Add to her depression the fatigue she was experiencing as her body grew to house those three heartbeats, thirty fingers and thirty toes. Plus, all the hormonal changes which fuelled her agitation and worries around the C-section birth which for triplets can cause a multitude of problems. The emotional pressure on my wife was immense. The way I saw it there was only one thing I could do to help her. Step back and be patient. Stop pressuring her to open to me. I also stopped giving her answers when she did want to talk because I knew she didn't really want them - it just pissed her off more. It was hard because it's the way I work - if something's broken I want to find a solution and fix it. My wife didn't want me to fix her - she just needed me to listen.

That little awareness of my need to fix and having the ability through the meditation practice to just step back was enough to take some of the pressure off our potential fireball of a relationship during that time. It still saves tension now. My whole approach to my wife and her moods had to change during the pregnancy – I had to be aware she was not feeling like her usual self. There was a sense of 'where's my wife gone?' on many occasions. At times I feared she's never come back, a fear that would rear its ugly head further down the road.

One night early into the second trimester we were sat up in bed watching TV. She had been agitated with me since I had got home from work. I asked her what was up, and she got angry, then burst into tears that turned into hysterical laughing, then back to inconsolable crying, then back to laughing while I sat looking at her bemused and slightly concerned. Waiting perhaps for her head to start spinning and the pea soup to spray all over the sheets. She said she felt relieved and much better afterwards (as did I that she wasn't possessed and simply pregnant). There were many such emotional outbursts over the months as her body stretched and broke to facilitate our growing family. All I could do was stand back when I needed to and keep loving her.

Our talk at the city hospital left some weight on my shoulders. The realisation that I could not let her down hit me every day. I also needed to be aware of the emotional adjustments that Frankie was going to experience and was already feeling the pinch of. It was not just my wife and I that were under pressure. Children have strange ways of dealing with stress if they have no way to explain what they feel. Frankie feared that these babies would be loved more than her. As she would put it to me 'they will be your real daughters'. It was tough to hear this from her. Frankie is the type of child that doesn't like to upset or hurt anyone's feelings. This makes it hard for her to initiate any important conversations she may want to have. I made the point of regularly talking to her about how she was feeling, letting her know how she would be involved, how much her sisters would look up to her and how much we loved her.

Stacey and I expected a few changes in her attitudes and behaviours, and they came as jealousy caught up with her occasionally. I have made it a part of my commitment to her as her Dad to teach her about the principles of love, tolerance and patience. She understands what jealousy is (just one of the many forms of anger) and how it can affect someone who holds on to it. She knows how to let go of anger because I have shown her how to meditate. She knows how to forgive others - and as importantly how to forgive herself. For the most part of the pregnancy she understandably clung to her Mum. They both had common ground with their insecurities, and Frankie became her mother's carer for no other reason than she wanted to.

Our father-daughter relationship took a bit of a hit during that time. If she played up and I pulled her up on it, she would run straight to mum who would let her get away with most things. I think in a way Stacey was experiencing guilt and worry over Frankie which is why she went against me around discipline during those months. Again, it was understandable. It brought tension and caused a few problems in the home, but they were resolved like most of our problems - by having sensible, honest conversations without bitterness or rancour with each other. Those were – like most of our chats picked at appropriate times when we were both less on edge.

I had another creeping doubt that began rearing its head during the second trimester, one I felt unable to discuss comfortably with my wife as I didn't want to potentially worry her with more concerns than she was already carrying. It was my past mental health and my concern of how much of it may be hereditary. My wife is fully aware of my past, and although none of it has carried through to be a problem in our relationship so far, it is a past I cannot shut the door on.

The emotional conflicts I had struggled with from sexual abuse as a child began to crop up from nowhere at the prospect of being a parent, it was a horrible thing to have to think about. There was also the past diagnosis of Borderline Personality Disorder, Asperger's Syndrome as well as a paranoid schizophrenic episode which left a very dark hole in my life. Although I no longer suffered the damaging effects and thinking from most of those symptoms, I couldn't help cringing each time I recalled one of the many conversations I had had with professionals who had suggested that I probably inherited a lot of those conditions. Genetic bullets if you like. Ones that I hoped with everything in me would not be passed on to any of my children.

It is one of the reasons I feared becoming a dad in the past. That and my total lack of responsibility towards myself and others. A part of me felt it would be a cruel stroke of fate to pass on to an unsuspecting child the problems that had continually hampered and all but destroyed my life and hurt many others that I met along the way.

It was during the process of getting sober that I discovered the nature, and subsequently the cause of my problems. Not just the alcoholism in fact but also the deteriorating mental health symptoms I had experienced throughout my life. It was one of the biggest most liberating 'A-Ha' moments of my life. I had discovered a single cause of my problems. And although trauma had a part to play – it wasn't those events that were the main problem. The anger I was holding onto around those events that had pierced me was causing the real problems. Resentment and my inability to deal with stressful situations in the stream of life was destroying me from the inside out. Everything else like the depression and anxiety were just symptoms of the internal conflict of suppressing those negative emotions.

It is this understanding of my past that has brought me to my current state of awareness. I don't believe I was born with any mental health problems. I believe much of what I was told by well-meaning professionals was wrong. Neither was I born with an inclination toward alcoholism which is another false narrative I have sat through many times in my life. As for the Asperger's? I will have to wait and see. Autism and ADHD do run in my family. Perhaps there is a genetic neurological difference that runs through generations of my family line - or maybe there isn't. The one thing I am certain of is that resentment/anger is an invisible electric force that gets passed on through families. It's like a rotten thread running unknowingly through our emotions - transferred through impatience, bitterness, hatred, jealousy and fear from parents to their children.

My father's fear and resentments all but destroyed our family. His anger eventually became mine. I became everything I hated because of that unseen transference. I came to realise - as I saw it clearly for myself - that there was a lineage of spiritual sickness in my family that had to stop with me. If things were to change with me and how I approached the world and relationships; that spirit of anger I had harboured most of my life that drove my self-justified, self-centred lifestyle - had to be replaced by a spirit of love and patience. I now know that to become a good husband and parent, and to succeed in raising a strong healthy family unit, love and tolerance is not only needed but essential. Anger has no place in a home.

Only time would tell if my daughters would be affected by my biological heritage. Or if a patient and loving home, free from anger would be enough for them to thrive mentally emotionally and spiritually no matter what their personalities or needs. Worrying was pointless. It was just another tempting distraction from what was in front of me. I am however convinced that my children's wellbeing - and the wellbeing of all those under my roof is in proportion to my own. The ability to practice patience and bring emotional stability and consistency to my home is of the greatest importance as a husband and a father. How I am in myself effects everyone around me.

Chapter 12

A slow acceptance

As we crossed into the second trimester all three babies were developing without a hitch. It was as much a shock to us as it was a blessing. Although we were a long way from being out of the woods, the twins for the time being were sharing successfully and growing steadily together without any visible issues. One was slightly smaller but that was to be expected. The singleton, who was the largest, was also developing as well as a baby could. The chromosome tests all came back normal which was a weight off our minds. Even if any of the babies came back in the high percentage for Downs Syndrome, it would not have changed our minds about reducing. We had the tests to give us a chance to prepare for ourselves. With three there is more to plan for − there are so many possible outcomes. We didn't want any more surprises! For now, the babies were healthy and that was enough to keep us focused on the road ahead. That first twelve weeks had seemed like a total rollercoaster and even though we were still riding it, the initial shock had begun to wear off.

Home life changed for all of us as the weeks went on. My wife was able to do less and less as the second trimester progressed. The way the triplets were positioned meant she almost constantly had a baby pressing against her lungs. The shortest of walks or even a trip upstairs took all the energy out of her. Everything was becoming a struggle. As hard work as it was, I slowly took over most of the chores. From cleaning to cooking, shopping and anything else that needed doing. I enjoy cooking so I made a point of looking up different simple recipes which contained the essential vitamins and minerals my wife needed. Vegetables and proteins that would help her stay healthy and provide the babies with the nutrients they needed to help them develop. I was learning there was so much we could already do to give the babies the opportunity to grow strong and to raise their chances of survival. A big part of that was keeping my home a calming environment, as much as possible anyway! Not easy when I had a very pregnant woman exploding with hormones, baiting arguments and picking at everything I did to help, but I managed to stay relatively neutral. At times it was just for the sake of the triplets and Frankie that I bit my tongue and sucked down my pride. It wasn't easy for my wife either. She literally couldn't control her emotions and I could see that. What she was going through was for us and there were times I had to remind myself of that. Especially on the days I would come home from an exhausting day at work, cook for us all then go out to do the shopping. Get home and tidy the house only to be getting shouted at ten o'clock at night when I finally sat down because the skirting boards were not cleaned properly.

It's a fact that stress in a mother can complicate an unborn baby's development. I stayed awake to that knowledge every day. Biting my tongue didn't just avoid escalating arguments, it contributed to my growing Daughters health as they developed. Watching for the temptation to react and retaliate was vital during that time. Another case for why conscious awareness in oneself is so vital to the health of a family. I had to keep a level head.

Stacey's cravings were for the most part sporadic. I didn't need to head out each night at three am to buy random foods, which was what I was half expecting after hearing other Dads midnight mission tales. She would crave something like ice cream one day, and the next she would go off it and require something else to fix her needs, so Frankie and I got to feed on the abundance of left over ice cream, cookies and whatever else was filling the kitchen cupboards.

I'm going to share some advice that may save you an argument and a night on the sofa if you have a pregnant partner at home who has sent you to pick up any specific snacks or foods. I pride myself as someone who has initiative. I am the sort of man that in the past has turned up on a remote island off the north of Scotland with no money and set up my own little business and found enough work to support myself for a year, working as a valued part of the community. So, when I was sent to the shop to pick up a specific brand of chocolate chip mint ice cream, which the shop I drove to didn't stock, I felt confident in selecting a similar item that I foolishly thought would suffice. Bad idea! I should have called to explain said item wasn't available and offer other options, or at least driven around to find what she craved. My initiative was not appreciated when I arrived home. Thinking on my feet resulted up in a very upset wife and a TV remote being thrown at my head. Lesson learned. The dent in the wall served as a reminder.

Rather than react to her constant changes, instead I made more of an effort to be patient with her. There were little things I would do for her that she was now unable to do for herself. As a welder I have a steady hand, so I got good at painting her toenails. I took the time to do a good job of it. If it's something you are going to attempt my best advice would be to use a good quality varnish as you don't want to be messing about with two coats. And go slowly. Trust me, she'll love you for it and it may save you from another night on the sofa being bombarded with texts messages reminding you that "it's all your fault she's like this".

There was one odd craving she developed which became a daily fix, one she had also had when carrying Frankie. She began chewing sponges at night. Little bath sponges to be specific, they needed to be a certain type with certain texture. There was nothing she loved more at the end of the day then chewing on a sponge. I found it bizarre, but I understand uncontrollable cravings with a past of alcoholism, and if the lady carrying our triplets needed to chew sponges, she got sponges.

There was one instance I took the initiative on that was a positive move for both of us. Firstly - because I felt it my duty to do so. Secondly - because I wanted my wife to have confidence in me as a father to the triplets. I made a point and a show of bonding with them. By the second trimester Stacey had become more comfortable with the three growing babies. I was also allowed to refer to them now as the triplets without it upsetting her. It was also at that time we felt the first kicks, to place a hand on my wife's bump and feel those little punches - kicks and tiny movements - was surreal. I would lie next to her in awe that the woman I married now had four heartbeats in that one body. It was a phenomenal experience to be a part of.

In the mornings before I went to work, I would kiss her bump and say goodbye to the babies. And in the evening, I used to get books from Frankie's room and read to them. There were times I was tired and felt silly doing it, and times my wife wasn't in the mood for me talking to her bump, but I persisted. I also played them music. As a musician with a passion for sound I made sure they were exposed to some tasty guitar riffs and sweet soul music. We played them classical, blues, jazz, rock. It was a way for me to personally connect in my own way. I can't stress how important my show of interest was in those babies. My wife had been let down by men. She was now going through the biggest physical and emotional event she would probably experience while on this earth and I wanted her to see that I was going nowhere. That I was going to be involved and love these babies before they even took their first breaths.

I hoped that from me putting the work in she would get confidence enough to know I meant business, and although I had never changed a nappy in my life, I was already stepping into my role. Bonding was for my benefit also. I have worked with and known men who grew to resent their children before they were even born. Incoming stresses such as the looming home life changes, the financial pressures, relationship strains and the woman's focus shifting to the baby can cause jealousy and bitterness to take hold. The most common symptom of suppressed anger is depression. Sadly, when the baby is seen as the problem the disconnect felt by the father towards the child can be too much to bridge. That relationship can be damaged forever unless he rediscovers lost consciousness. I was aware that my wife's focus was shifting from me, even more so with the anxiety she was experiencing. I was already feeling a bit alienated under my roof as Stacey and Frankie strengthened their bond. It was difficult not to let self-pity creep in at times, but I saw it was what they both needed to do, and besides - it wasn't about me. I can easily see how a person can grow to resent the people they love. I couldn't let this happen to me. Allowing resentment to get in was a trap I had to constantly navigate around in the daily emotional tides of the pregnancy. The temptation to react with pride and anger came on a regular basis. I knew the consequences of me becoming overwhelmed would affect all my family.

Bonding with the triplets kept my feet on the ground and reinforced my sense of purpose as dad. There were times at home it felt with the triplets like 'us and them'. Stacey would joke that if we ever split up as a couple, she would take Frankie and I would get the triplets to deal with. And although she was joking, I sensed an underlying seriousness from her. There were quite a few running jests and comments along those lines. I took them on the chin and carried on with what I felt was the right thing to be doing. After all I was practically winging my whole part, based mostly on what I had learned from my failures in life because of no real fatherly guidance of my own. I knew though that bonding was as important with a father to a child as it was with a mother. My role was equally as important to my children. And I wanted my daughters to grow up knowing that from the start.

The slow acceptance from Stacey around having triplets now opened the door to an all-important set of discussions. What sex they may be and what names to give them. My wife and Frankie wanted all girls. This would mean a house full of women and me (and the dog). This possible outcome was probably the most daunting to face as a man, and a first-time biological father. I liked the idea of twin boys and a girl. This would balance up the siblings nicely. Two boys and two girls seemed fair to everyone. I think every man would like at least one son to raise, I do think men understand men better - and women understand women better!

Choosing names became a nightmare. We had to settle on three boy's names and three girls. From those six we had to eliminate one or two from each sex depending on the various outcome and both be happy with the one boy's or girls name. In short it got frustrating. Mostly because we would settle on great names, then the next day Stacey would change her mind completely after finding new ones. After much discussion, there were a couple we both liked, agreed on and stuck to. For the time being though the triplets became affectionately known as the twins and odd Bob. It was the Eighteen-week scan in the city that we first discovered the sex of the twins. Odd Bob was positioned too awkwardly to be able to tell that day.

Dr Dean welcomed us through to the scanning room. I felt

we had developed a good relationship with him as our doctor as the weeks went on. I always felt like I was being tested by him at those visits. It was like he wanted to be sure I was taking care of my wife and Frankie, and that my feet were firmly on the ground and I was taking it all seriously. We met other parents at the hospital who didn't care for him very much. It would have been quite easy to have taken his questioning and forwardness with me as insulting, but it wasn't. This man knew exactly what we were facing and wanted me looking at the same picture, he knew only too well I needed to be strong for my family, no matter what the outcome.

He positioned the camera on Stacey's bump and moved it quickly and with precision to see that all was doing what it should be. I had the usual anticipation going into the examination, it always rapidly dissipated with the report from the Dr of three strong heartbeats. He checked for their organ development, measured their heads and checked their brains for any abnormalities. He was visibly impressed that the triplets had all reached eighteen weeks without problems.

My wife asked if he was able to tell us the sex. He slid the camera around, pressing it, his face concentrating on the screen in front. I sat excitedly with bated breath, holding my wife's hand. He congratulated us and announced that the twins were girls. Unfortunately, he was unable to see the relevant bits of the singleton. My wife was over the moon and I saw a glimmer of relief in her eyes for the first time in a long time. I was also happy, twin girls I figured may be easier to deal with further down the line than boys. Plus, I could still have a son. I may not be completely outnumbered yet. A decision was made that day that it would be in our interest to let the city hospital take over all the fortnightly scans until we were out of the risk zone of twin to twin transfusion or any other serious complications. That would be around twenty-seven weeks. It meant more uncomfortable trips for my wife, but it was for the best, as our Doctor put it, "we don't want to miss anything from here on in".

Chapter 13

Calm before a storm

The physical strain on my wife was taking a real toll coming into the warmer months. Getting her out and about became near impossible without a mobility aid. We ended up borrowing a wheelchair for shopping, or any outings that could involve walking any distance. Every week she took a 'bumpy' photo in the mirror to document her physical growth in pictures and it was scary to see how fast she got big. By the second trimester she had developed an iron deficiency purely from the amount of blood she was producing for the growing babies. Her abdominal muscles split from the outward pressure of the bump, and the shortness of breath got worse as the babies squashed against her lungs. She was lucky that her blood pressure remained normal throughout the pregnancy.

I had to help her stand up from a sitting position and she was unable to get in and out of the bath without my help. Frankie did all she could to help her Mum. She would help her get dressed after baths, rub moisturising cream into her bump and keep her happy with a constant supply of juice so she didn't dehydrate. Frankie is a real mother-hen and loved being of use to her Mum, it kept them both close in all the uncertainty surrounding us. We were heading into a heat wave and a long hot summer which wouldn't help my wife's discomfort.

The days were a balance of my day job and caretaking at home. We slowly got the bits and pieces we would need for the babies' arrival. Getting a little bit off our list each month helped to take some of the financial pressure off. I had an extra cupboard put in under the stairs amongst other little jobs, we would need as much storage space as possible. We could have gone crazy, panic buying for things we may need for three babies, but with just sticking to the essentials we figured we would buy as we needed when they arrived, rather than needlessly spend money. Stacey's relatives had been donating some of the equipment like a Moses basket and baby bath that was kept from the last baby born in her family. We kept our sights as much as possible on a positive outcome with the triplets and planned with that in mind. It was crucial to stay focused on what needed doing and staying awake to the rising doubts of what may or may not occur in the coming weeks. It was a reality of the pregnancy that we could lose any of the babies at any time. We had to be prepared for that happening at some level but not let it overtake us emotionally. For the time being it was nothing but a possibility.

At the twenty-week scan we were met at the hospital by Stacey's Mother and both her older sisters. I was still pinning my hopes on a son, even Frankie had decided that after finding out she had another two sisters on the way it would be nice to have a baby brother, she thought it would be especially nice for me too. Our good Doctor ushered us all into the room, began with the scan and proceeded taking the usual measurements and checking the vitals. It was a tense moment for me especially.

With the previous news to the family of twin girls, almost everyone we knew had hopes for news of a boy that day. Dr Dean finished his checks and began the search for a penis at my request. He eventually stopped moving the camera, looked at me with an apologetic half smile and said, "Sorry, you have three girls, I'd suggest you start drinking". Stacey was thrilled that she would now have four daughters, as were her sisters. I had a momentary feeling of deflation that quickly passed. The fact that so far, we had three babies with strong heartbeats growing without any complications overshadowed any preconception about what sex they were. I can honestly say I walked out of that scan room feeling proud. It seemed God felt I had much to learn from raising four daughters (either that or he has a great sense of humour). Frankie was the most disappointed, but she soon came around to the news. I was to be outnumbered five to one. As a good friend pointed out when he was done laughing on hearing my news, it was either going to sharpen me - or kill me. From that day on the triplets were known as our three little birds. The names we settled on were 'Ava' for the singleton, 'Blakely' for the smaller twin and 'Lacey' was the last name chosen for the larger of the two. Beautiful names that we both fully agreed on, and with the names came even more of sense of realness around the pregnancy.

*

Raising daughters was going to be a challenge without a doubt. After all, I will be the man they judge all other men by, and that's a huge responsibility however you dress it up. If ever I felt a need to improve myself as a human being it came with knowing I would be a father to four little ladies. My role in their lives would be one I could not fail at. If anything, my sense of purpose was strengthened with the knowledge of a future raising daughters, and what they would need to see in me as a father to each of them. The relationship I had with Stacey was the first one I had ever had sober and free from mental health problems. With sobriety I had come to realise the vital need I had for a guiding moral compass in my life.

When the past self-centred existence I had cultivated finally ran its course, I awoke to the truth of my failings. And with those truths saw that if my future was to be different from my past I would have to start on a new footing. The way I treated others had to change, and as a parent then to Frankie I had to be an example. I don't imagine there is a parent out there who doesn't experience guilt or shame from time to time at memories they cringe at and would rather brush under the rug. With a past of alcoholism, violence and psychiatric problems, I had a truckload. But I couldn't let my past dictate my future. If I continued making excuses for myself and not working to become a better human being because of fear and guilt left over from a poorly lived past, my children would just end up victims of my excuses. I would be no better than I was when I drank. Yes, I have made many mistakes during my life, I have hurt many people and have done things I am not proud of. But I have also now become a parent - and with that position there comes a responsibility to my children to improve towards a better ideal, no matter what my past. Guilt, as it turns out, has been my saving grace. It is the force working through my consciousness that has encouraged me to make changes and strive for a better existence for myself and ultimately those who rely on me. And I had reached a time in my life where moving forward was not only an appropriate thing to do, but a matter of necessity If I was to live and succeed whilst raising a healthy and successful family.

There was a growing mix of anxiousness and relief as the examinations passed without any problems. Later in the pregnancy we had both found triplet parent sites through social media. These sites were a blessing to us. For the first time we had an opportunity to connect with others on the same path and read about others' experience. We soon discovered that those sites can also create more worry if you're inclined to panic. Not everyone has a smooth ride with triplets. From developing twin to twin transfusion, parents losing babies, and reading first-hand the stresses of parents who were thrown into life with multiples. We knew the struggles were real. It could get a little overwhelming to read the negative side as well as the positive realities of multiples, so it was important for me to keep my sights on our situation. As an English man I was surprised to find the only sites accessible to me were in the U.S. There was hardiness within that community of Dads that I related to, I respected them. What became clear from joining that community was that the road ahead was going to get tough. I found no nonsense support and encouragement. One of the first pieces of advice I was given was to not split up from - or divorce my wife in the first year, no matter what. It was another wake-up call for me, another conscious moment of realisation about the gravity of what may be ahead. So, to get through each scan without issues was to us a growing miracle. It was clear from reading other's experiences that my wife and I had much to be grateful for.

At the twenty-eight week scan we made the last

uncomfortable trip to Bristol. The heatwave was in full force and my wife was glad it would be the last trip. She was done with the travelling. The Dr completed his checks, pushed his chair back, spun and looked at us both with a big smile – "This is just remarkable, we would have chewed our arms off to get you to twenty-four weeks. Whatever it is you've done to get here has worked, well done both of you".

To hear this from him brought a massive sense of relief and achievement. We were now at least in the clear from twin to twin transfusion. If it hadn't happened by now, it would no longer be a danger to any of the girls, or my wife. The twins had managed to successfully share a placenta - they had beaten the odds to both develop normally. After a short momentary celebration, it was back to business. As the Dr pointed out, the next bit was to avoid an emergency labour, which could happen at any moment and for them all to enter the world screaming. Stacey was to have two steroid shots before the arrival date to strengthen the trio's lungs. He was happy for our local hospital, who were also delivering them to now take over the rest of the scans. We left our final meeting with Dr Dean sharing a mutual respect.

The final weeks however brought a major problem, particularly for my wife. Up until two weeks before our elected birth date the plan had been to have the babies delivered in our local hospital. My wife was comfortable with this as she knew it well and, as I mentioned before, had herself been born on the same maternity ward, as had Frankie. We had visited the Special care baby unit (SCBU) and met with some of the nurses who worked on the ward on a previous visit.

As far as we knew everything was arranged and in place for us to have the triplets in the local hospital until the day that we met the head pediatrician, who had up until that point cancelled several prior appointments with us. A few weeks before that day we had met the anesthetist who went through the whole procedure with Stacey so she had a clear understanding of what would happen during the day of the babies' arrival. We had no reason to expect any issues with the hospital.

Our Specialist seemed agitated when we arrived. We had never known him not full of smiles and confidence and it was clear there was a problem. He warned us that he didn't think the hospital now wanted to do the triplet's delivery. We were asked to wait in a side room where we would be met by the head pediatrician and our doctor would join us after.

I felt Stacey's nerves building as we waited. I tried to calm her but was feeling a little on edge myself waiting to hear what they had to say. The pediatrician came in and wasted no time in giving us the news. They were not confident in performing the C-section. They explained that it was too high risk. If one or all of them were born with difficulties it would mean transporting one or all of them to separate, larger hospitals to be treated. We could end up with three ill babies in three separate hospitals scattered around the south of England. It would be a logistical nightmare for us to deal with. The added risk to that outcome was physically transporting them. There was a specialist unit that operated out of Bristol with a custom-built ambulance and crew for transporting new-born babies, but they could only facilitate moving one at a time. In short, having the babies delivered at our local hospital came with too much risk.

Stacey was devastated to hear all this at the last minute while already suffering anxiety around the C-section. We asked if we could have them delivered in Bristol at the hospital that dealt with our scans, but they had already called St Michaels and we were refused as they saw our triplets as low risk compared to other cases they had to deal with. Had there been any visible difficulties during the last scans, especially concerning any heart or organ development problems - Bristol would have taken them. They are a specialist baby unit, specially equipped for complicated arrivals. But our three little birds were looking healthy as could be.

We were then told that staff at the Musgrove hospital in Taunton were more than happy to deliver our trio. It was a large hospital, well equipped to deal with any emergencies that may happen on arrival day. The triplets and my wife would be in good hands. I knew the hospital, and although it was a bit of a drive, I was happy that they were confident in taking us, and as we were told, excited to be delivering our triplets into the world.

My wife was not happy at all. She was shaking with anger and there was nothing I was able to say to help her see that it was going to be for the best. I mean, who wants their babies brought into the world by doctors who are not confident to do so? It was a procedure that required confidence and skill. Her upset was not so much at the move of hospital, but at the last-minute announcement. Their reasons for not wanting to go ahead with our delivery were reasons they would have been aware of all along. They told us they would only now take us in an emergency. Which was the last thing we wanted

All our doctor could do was apologise. I felt bad for him, and not just because my wife was a formidable force at the best of times during the pregnancy and he was now to feel the full brunt of her discontent, but more-so because it seemed like our doctor had been stumped by a decision from above that he ultimately had no say in. It was arranged that we would meet the pediatricians at Musgrove the following week. It would at least give us a chance to get familiar with the place. The one request we had that was all agreed on was that as soon as the triplets were born, if they were all without complication they would be moved straight back to our local hospital. This would make life easier for us as it was just down the road from our home. It would eliminate a lot of travel and be simpler for us to get Frankie to school and back.

To say Stacey felt anxious around the C-section would be an understatement. She was terrified that something could go wrong and that she would lose her life. She told me in those last few weeks that she wasn't worried about the triplets, she was afraid that Frankie may lose another biological parent. We had both read horror stories about multiple birth C-sections and we knew there was a high risk of complications. I never told my wife, but I read an article during the last weeks of our pregnancy covering the story of a woman who had lost both her legs due to hemorrhaging and other serious complications during the procedure. It was just more temptation to get lost in fear and my wife was experiencing enough of that. The meditation kept me out of the doubts and worries. After all, everything about our pregnancy was high risk and we had got this far. I was confident we were in good hands at Musgrove hospital. Their Maternity and Neo Natal Intensive Care Unit had an excellent reputation. That was all I needed to know.

We had our final scan on the Friday at Musgrove. We were able to meet some of the team who would be involved with the arrival on the following Monday. Once again, we had to sit through all the possible problems and outcomes that could occur during the C-section and as before it was hard to hear but it was just procedure on their part. I liked the nurses we met. They were excited to be delivering our three little birds which gave me confidence. Stacey was still noticeably unhappy about the whole move of hospital but felt better with the news that a female surgeon would be performing the surgery. She again enquired about a natural birth which would have been her wish but was told again that the dangers would be ten-fold.

Stacey's Mum who was with us that day and had now moved in to help us out was hoping to be present at the birth. Unfortunately, it was explained to us that the theatre would be packed that day with the three separate teams for each baby, plus all the other doctors and technicians who would usually be there. Stacey was allowed one person with her and she asked that it was me, and I wasn't going to miss it for the world after the rollercoaster we had been on to get there. I knew it was upsetting for Stacey's mum. She was concerned for her daughter, which was her main reason for wanting to be there on the day, and I understood that.

We were taken through the events awaiting us the following Monday and asked that we be there for seven thirty am, to be in theatre for eight thirty am. The triplets just needed to stay where they were for the next three nights. No one wanted the stress of an emergency labour or surgery. I began to feel a real sense of apprehension after that last scan. I was praying for three healthy babies to enter the world without too much drama or any serious complications to my wife, and that when they were born, she would bond with them. I was unaware of the extent of the detachment she felt from the three lives growing inside of her. She assured me that once she saw them the way she felt would all change.

The heat was stifling in the house that last weekend. The fans hummed twenty-four seven to try and push some air through, any relief was welcomed by Stacey. Frankie and I filled the paddling pool on the Saturday morning, and we made a makeshift shelter in the garden so that Stacey could sit out in the shade and rest her swollen feet in the cool water. It became a weekend of reflection. It still didn't seem real that in a couple of days our family would double in size and I would begin the journey of fatherhood from scratch as a multiple parent. As for Stacey, she was just glad that the pregnancy would be over. We have a photo of her standing in the living room that weekend holding her bump. Her face says it all, she had well and truly had enough.

Looking back over the last thirty-three weeks there was much I had to be grateful for, as hard as it had been. The triplets had all developed without issues and even with polycystic ovary syndrome my wife had successfully carried them safely. The chance of us even conceiving triplets naturally was remote. Only around 120 sets are born every year in the U.K, and of those many face ongoing complications and the survival rate in the first year is lower in triplets. But they are also stronger to develop in the womb, I guess from having to fight for space. For the developing mono twins, it literally becomes a fight for survival; multiple babies are tough little cookies.

For me, the pregnancy felt like the ultimate test of my position as a husband to Stacey and a Father to Frankie. My hope was that through my consistency they had both gained strength in the times they felt the lowest. And that they also saw in me a man who was going nowhere, who was ready for the road ahead and willing to be what they needed me to be. Even though it was stressful, I never really lost my faith in the situation we had been given. The sense of purpose I felt from the start, and the excitement I felt all the way through brought me a natural positivity. I didn't need to willfully pretend to my family that I was confident and okay, I just was. There was a grace surrounding the pregnancy and one I felt in myself. I had managed to stay present for the most of it. I had avoided getting overwhelmed by the many fears and doubts within me.

My wife, further down the line, told me that as tough as it was for her the one thing that she got relief from during those months while she was suffering was knowing that I was doing okay, and that she didn't need to worry about me. She knew I was conscious enough to see past her anger and anxieties to know that there was nothing was personal in her attitude towards me. When she told me this, it was a comfort to know that my intuition during the pregnancy was right. The principles of love, patience and tolerance from me was enough of a foundation to get us through as a family - and as a couple. It gave me a confidence looking at the road ahead. A little faith was going to go a long way.

It was a weekend one of quiet gratitude. I felt stronger than ever in the light of what we had all achieved as a family. Frankie was excited. My wife was nervous about the delivery but looking forward to not carrying the huge weight of three babies, two placentas and two sacs full of fluid. She was exhausted and just wanted them out. It was a lazy weekend in the sun, though I was never far away from the feeling we were in the calm before a storm.

There are no words to describe the respect I have for Stacey. For what she went through for all us during the first half of that year. Reflecting, I had one priority and duty, to support my wife no-matter what. Everything else came secondary to her wellbeing. I was on the other side, dealing with someone with depression and anxiety, and when someone is that overwhelmed, helping them to see the light can seem impossible. I had to resist the urge to constantly try and fix her while she was in that darkness, as painful as it was to watch and frustrating as it was at times knowing I had a solution that could help her by way of meditation, I knew any willful effort to help her would have only have pushed her to sink further. It wasn't about any fears I had for us and what I may have wanted. I needed just to be patient with her, in the hope that If I could remain solid, she would meet me again on the other side. Whenever it was that she got there.

Chapter 14

Three little birds

Monday the fourth of July 2017.

There have been very few life changing moments that I knew were coming, or at best that I was granted any opportunity to mentally prepare for. That's why it pays to live consciously in the stream of life. The unexpected is always around the corner - so to be awake when it hits, is the only real defence against the emotional smack in the face some of these events can deliver.

I felt I was as prepared as a man can be on the early morning of our delivery date. We were packed ready for the hospital and set to go. Stacey was understandably quiet and nervous. I was excited - and Frankie too. The plan was to drop Frankie at her Aunties who would then take her to school. We felt it best she wasn't there for the delivery in case of any problems. Stacey's sister would then bring her in later that afternoon when hopefully things were settled and when more of the family would be visiting. My Mother-in-law drove, and Stacey rode shotgun up front. Not much was said on the hour-long journey to the hospital. We were all feeling the anticipation. I was watching my wife from the back seat.

Just looking at the woman I loved who was soon to become a mother of four, I was in awe of her. Within the next couple of hours, the triplets would be joining us into the world, it was hard to take in. As we drove, I was being hit with memories of other pivotal moments in my life that had changed my path forever. I enjoyed that car ride, it was a peaceful hour. I had the feeling nothing was going to be peaceful in my life again - at least for a while!

We arrived a little early. There was a slight hill from the car park to the Maternity ward and pushing that wheelchair with my wife up it was a real workout for me. I was glad it was the final push. We had time to grab a coffee on the way in and then we waited to be called through from the waiting room. I could see the nerves bubbling in Stacey and her mum. I was excited but also aware of how they were feeling so I contained myself and kept cool. Soon after arriving we were called into the secured ward and taken into a side room with a single bed. My wife was asked to put on a hospital gown as the nurse spoke with her and asked questions about the current positions of the babies. She jotted down the information and went through some routine forms. We were again explained the risks and Stacey was asked to sign a consent form prior to the procedure. While Stacey was getting ready, I was asked to go with another nurse to put my scrubs on. I changed in a tiny room with a few lockers against the wall and a selection of different size white boots to wear into theatre. I took the opportunity of a moment alone to say a prayer, I asked God for the only thing I ever ask for, to give me the strength to deal with whatever may come. My chest was expanding with adrenalin and fear as I got myself ready to go. The nurse came back in the room with a pad, flipped it open and asked me the names of each of the triplets. I knew each baby by their size. I knew Ava was the biggest, Lacey was the bigger twin and Blakely was the smallest of the three. She wrote it all down and explained that they would know who each baby was as they were born, and for us not to worry about them getting mixed up. We also had little hats knitted for each of them to help with any confusion. It was something Stacey and I had talked about quite a bit beforehand, the 'what if they muddle them up'? conversation. I imagine it's a conversation many a couples with multiples have before they arrive. The nurse came across as confident and reassured us both that we were all in good hands.

I returned to the room where my wife was. She was shaking with nerves and her mum was also anxious from seeing her daughter so worried. I will never get used to seeing her as overwhelmed with anxiety as she was during the pregnancy. The waves of fear kept hitting her and that morning was no different.

There was one more surprise for my wife before we went

through to theatre, one that upset her further. We were expecting a woman to be performing the procedure, but when the surgeon entered the room, instead we were met by an enormous smiling Ghanaian doctor with hands like spades. My wife was visibly upset by the last-minute change in plan and I could see he felt just as awkward picking up on her strange reaction. It was just another unexpected change and it threw her. She asked him how many triplets he had delivered but he wouldn't give her a straight answer - he said it was irrelevant. That was enough for my wife to start crying.

It was strange being pumped with so much excitement and adrenalin and once again, seeing my poor wife experiencing the complete opposite. There was no going back now though, the ball was rolling. The time quickly came to go through to theatre. Stacey's mum was hugging her and comforting her as we left the room. I had only ever seen her mum twice with a tear in her eye. Once at the wedding when I gave a ring to Frankie and again that morning when we left the room. I felt bad that she was not able to be with us, but neither could I give her my place. I wasn't going to miss seeing my daughters come into this world for anything.

It was a big theatre and we had already been told that there would be quite a few people present and not to let that overwhelm us. As we walked down the corridor and into the room we were met with an excited crowd of nurses and technicians. There were three open cots along one side of the room. Each had a baby's name on a piece of paper attached to it. Each cot had a doctor, a pediatrician and a midwife stood with it. The atmosphere was electric. I was asked to sit on a stool, neatly tucked in besides Stacey's upper half surrounded with wires and equipment, holding my wife's shaking hand as the room vibrated with people. The next moment the doors swung open and a surge of more doctors and technicians rolled in. I counted eighteen people in that theatre, not including us. It was an impressive show for our girls.

It was at our request that music was played during the procedure. We had chosen Bob Marley's 'Three Little Birds' which was played on repeat, a song we had played to the triplets in utero regularly at home. As soon as the music started the whole room began moving to the rhythm, with people dancing and singing along. It was a moving moment that such a show was in place for our girl's big arrival. I will never forget the theatre that morning, or the atmosphere that was present. Not just for the reason we were there, but for the sense of joy and love that the triplets would enter the world to. It was simply beautiful.

Stacey was positioned, sat on the edge of the bed for the epidural injection. Looking at her in so much fear in a room full of so much excitement is what kept a foot on the ground for me; there was so much that could go wrong in the next few moments but also so much that could go right. Adrenalin continued pumping around my body as the surgeon and technicians prepared for the C-section. A sheet was placed just below Stacey's chest, so she was unable to see what was happening. One of the technicians asked if we had a camera or phone handy, she was kind enough to offer to take a few photos; to capture the moments the triplets left the cramped confines of the womb and took their first hits of oxygen. I was looking directly into my wife's eyes, reassuring her, telling her I loved her and how proud I was of her, that she was strong and we would be okay no matter what, I kept repeating myself over and over to try and give her some comfort. She could hardly speak, her voice broken with fear and her hands were shaking as she gripped mine tightly.

She asked me when they would be starting the procedure, a kind smiling technician leaned down and told us that they already had begun and to watch above the partition sheet. In the next moment a baby was lifted into the air, the twisted umbilical cord still attached, her arms stretched out straight to the sides like a bird stretching her wings in freedom for the first glorious time. In that instant my heart stopped - my breathing stopped. Everything stood still. I was looking at Ava for the first time. The tears began running down my face as her cord was cut and she let out a cry as they placed her on the open cot to be cleaned and given oxygen. She was out, alive and breathing, and the relief and joy I felt was overwhelming. Stacey looked at me and smiled for the first time that day at the sound of our daughter working her lungs out while the midwife and team cleaned her up. Exactly two minutes later Blakely was pulled into the world, visibly smaller than Ava as we already knew, but just as vocal as we prayed she would be.

Two were out and breathing well. Another two minutes past and Lacey was now with us. She too let out a high-pitched cry at the shock of leaving her first home in this world. The room kept buzzing with excitement as Ava was brought over and placed on Stacey's chest. Lacey and Blakely were then brought over one at a time with their little hats on, wrapped in white towels. Their little faces were beautiful. They passed each of them to me and I held their tiny frames for the first time. Stacey's face was beginning to show signs of relief that the babies were out and okay, and that she seemed to have gotten through it without complication. We later learned she had lost litres of blood and was given a transfusion, and that her uterus wouldn't contract and had to be manually squeezed back into place by hand which caused her a lot of pain when the medication wore off. But there was no panic in the room from anyone, it was all efficiently taken care of without us being aware of any problems.

One of the memories Stacey has of the C-section was our surgeon bobbing up and down in rhythm to Bob Marley while he smiled down at us and stitched her up. I was called over to the cots and asked if I would like to trim their umbilical cords back as they had been left long during the procedure of their exiting. It was another moment that strengthened my bond with the triplets. My hand has never been steadier. Ava was born at 9.37am weighing 4lb 12oz, Blakely at 9.39am weighing 3lb 4oz and Lacey at 9.41am weighing in at 4lb.7oz. And we were soon to discover - identical.

So that was it over. The triplets had arrived after a pregnancy with no complications to enter the world all screaming. God had graced us with three healthy babies who were already making waves with their arrival. After a short time of holding each one with my wife, they were taken through to another room to be checked over thoroughly by the doctors and moved on to the Neo-natal intensive care unit to be closely monitored. Lacey was off the oxygen almost immediately and holding her own. Ava and little Blakely needed a bit more support to begin with. Stacey was cleaned up and just before we left the surgeon said to her with a smile "you were my third set of triplets". He and everyone in that theatre had done a phenomenal job in taking care of us and the babies and in keeping the whole situation calm. It was one of the most moving hours of my life, nothing has shifted and lit up my consciousness more. When I held my daughters, I experienced an unconditional love for another human I had never felt before. It was a pure conscious connection - a spiritual bond. As a Father I knew that whatever happened now during my time here on earth I could not fail them. Moving forward and growing towards love as a human being had to become my priority for those who had been entrusted to me, for all those under my roof.

My wife and I returned to the recovery room where her Mum was waiting. Stacey was relieved it was all over and was given a chance to rest as the medication slowly wore off. I was feeling a huge sense of relief when we got back to the room, the adrenalin had begun slowing down in my body and my mind felt calmer. I didn't waste time in announcing the news to all the friends and family that we knew were waiting anxiously on the end of the phones for any updates. The response from everyone was that of relief and excitement. The weight was finally off, not just literally from Stacey, but collectively everyone close to us who had been involved with our journey, and all the friends watching from the side lines. Everyone could now relax a little.

Frankie was called while at school. The whole class and all the teachers were waiting anxiously for the phone to ring. She was so excited to come in and see us all after school, her relief was mostly that Mum was okay. It wasn't long before

Frank (my Father in law) turned up. His timing was perfect to go get a coffee as when he walked in Stacey's bowels opened as she had no sensation or control below. She was embarrassed the first time it happened, the second time – not so much. We took that as a good cue to leave and left her with her Mum and the nurse and took a little walk to the cafe to get some fresh air.

Frank has three daughters and is good to talk to about raising girls as someone who's been through it all. He was as amazed as everyone else around the whole triplet's deal. There was no history of any multiples we knew of on either side of our families which made it even more special. We walked and talked as the day began heating up and returned to the room just as a nurse came in with an update on the triplets and their weights. The report was positive, the girls were doing great and were now in the NICU and we would be free to visit them soon. The next plan of action was to move Stacey to a recovery ward where she would stay until discharged. We were in the room for a couple of hours before they were happy to move Stacey to the ward. Her legs were still shaky from the epidural and she was unable to walk, so her whole bed was moved to the new surroundings where we would be for the next few days.

It was a bustling ward filled with many new mums regaining their strength before leaving to begin their new lives. It wasn't a ward with rooms, but more of a long wide corridor with curtained partitions separating the beds. Nurses were dashing about with clipboards and notes, trolleys with food were rolling up and down the corridor as curtains were pulled back and forth protecting the privacy of the women on the ward. Stacey's bed was opposite a little kitchen with access to free coffee, so I was happy. We were also very close to the toilet and the secure entrance to the NICU ward which was helpful for my wife.

We packed Stacey's belongings away in the little bedside cupboards and made sure she was comfortable. Once a nurse had been in to take some notes and talk us through the ward, she offered to get a wheelchair for Stacey so we could go together to see our girls. Stacey felt too weak and although we offered to help her into the wheelchair from the bed, she felt she wasn't up to it just yet. I thought it was a bit odd that she passed up on the offer to go see them, but I also understood she was feeling rough after the morning she had just been through. She told us (her Mum and I) to go, that she would be fine and just needed to rest. I was excited to see them. I wanted to see their faces again. The nurse directed us on the walk through the maternity ward, past the labour rooms to the secure quiet calm of the NICU.

We pressed the intercom and I introduced myself proudly as the Dad of the triplets, and with a buzz the door clicked open. We entered a small corridor. To the right was a short walkway that led to the outdoor entrance which opened to a small enclosed garden. At the end of the corridor were two rooms and on the left was a naturally lit open room accommodating eight open cots - the next stage recovery ward after the NICU, where the stronger babies were moved to after incubation. There was a small nurse station in the centre, and the Mums and Dads were seated in reclining chairs by the cots enjoying taking care of their newborns.

The room to the right was the NICU ward. A similar sized ward as the one opposite with seven incubators placed around the central nurse's station. It was a quiet low-lit room with a side room like a small kitchen with fridges and a wash station for cleaning milk bottles. Just through the entrance there was a hand washing station. The only real noise in the room was the low decibel beeping from the monitors and the occasional running breast pump. A smiling nurse met us and explained the routine for entering the ward. The main concern was germ free hands. We had to wash them with soap and water and use the hand sanitizer each time we entered the ward and every time we left. It was the number one golden rule.

The three incubators in the far corner belonged to Ava, Lacey and Blakely. Ava's was the nearest to me. She was fast asleep within the warm glass. There were a few wires

162

attached to her monitoring her heart rate and a thin feeding tube running into her tiny mouth. She looked so peaceful as she slept. When I think of newly born premature babies I'm reminded of wrinkly little old men, weak and not quite formed. But Ava didn't look that way. She looked like a healthy strong baby, and she was beautiful. The nurse then showed me to the next incubator which housed Blakely. She had a few more wires than Ava and was still on oxygen. At 3lb 4oz she was a skinny little string bean. She too laid peacefully, her tiny hands clutched by her face between the wires as she rested. She was the smallest but still looked perfectly formed in her features. Lacey was laying on her belly, she was already off the oxygen and had fewer wires attached than her sisters. She looked perfect and comfortable.

Seeing them there for the first time resting in that peaceful environment was a humbling experience. I couldn't take my eyes off them, moving from one cot to another just soaking the moment in. I wished my wife was sharing that moment with me but knew she would be seeing them shortly. She too needed to gain her strength. I took a few photos of each of our daughters to show Stacey when I got back to her.

Stacey was in a lot of discomfort by this point, mainly from having her uterus manually contracted. As the afternoon went on visitors slowly arrived. Frankie turned up with her

Auntie Leesa, my mum and brother also came by, they were all itching to go and see the babies. The nurse taking care of Stacey asked her again if she would like to go with us to see them but as before she declined. I could understand it earlier in the day as her legs were genuinely numb from the C-section, but now I began to feel some concern generated by her seeming reluctance to go. She said again she was happy to stay and for us to carry on without her.

Frankie's face was a picture as she stood next to Ava's cot looking at her little sister lying sleeping. I was glad of her reaction as she moved between each cot. Frankie has always been sensitive to her Mum's emotions. Through the early days of the pregnancy it was if Frankie's reaction was always in reflection of her mum's. Gradually, as she saw Stacey begin to get to grips with the idea of triplets, Frankie's feelings shifted with her. Frankie's smile was beaming as I introduced her to her three little siblings and the rest of our visitors also switched between cots with excitement and relief. I have never seen my mum with such a look of pride and happiness. Stacey's sister and Di left us to get some photos developed to pin by Stacey's bed, up until then - apart from the short moment she saw them in the theatre - she had just seen photos on my phone.

As good as I was feeling on the surface, the longer the day went by the more I felt concern for my wife. There was at

164

least no physical reason for her to not come with me to see the babies. I didn't push the point; she was clearly experiencing an emotional conflict and needed space to process and not to be bothered with my worries.

The rest of that afternoon and evening was spent back and forth to the NICU. I was given some little knitted squares of wool by the nurse taking care of the girls, two for each baby. One was placed by each of the baby's heads, the other was kept in Stacey's top and were continually swapped each time I did a trip between them and mum. It was to comfort the babies by giving them a scent of their Mother. The visitors dwindled off by early evening and would be returning the next day. Frankie, myself and Di left at 10pm when the recovery ward finally quietened down and closed for visitors. We said our goodbyes to my exhausted wife and left for the journey home.

It had been a highly emotional day for all of us. It wasn't easy for me to leave that night; I just wanted to curl up with my wife and comfort her in my arms. On the drive home my stomach began sinking with a sense of dread as I stared out at the stars, my head swirling with thoughts as I came down heavily from the mental high. Drained by my own emotional exhaustion.

It hit me that after all the stress of the pregnancy we had just experienced that we could be now facing another rough time as a family with a situation I wasn't sure I had the strength left to deal with. Stacey had told me she felt absolutely no attachment to the triplets right the way through the pregnancy, a disconnect she assured me would dissolve the moment she saw them – but It was yet to happen. And I knew it could be a situation beyond anything I could fix. The thought that kept punching through as the worry swirled around my tired mind was that no matter what was coming; my daughters and my wife would need me to be strong - my faith needed to be strong. The triplets had made their entrance into the world and were going nowhere. I had to keep it together.

Chapter 15

Exhale

I woke up naturally the next morning around six am. My mind wasted no time in pulling up the concerns I went to sleep on. A quick meditation got me back to consciousness. I needed to be awake and aware of the fears I felt around Stacey not bonding with the triplets as it seemed it could now be a reality we had to face. I messaged Stacey to see if she was awake to talk. She got back quickly so I called - I was eager to talk to her. She had slept well, and a nurse had already offered to take her down to see the triplets once she had eaten breakfast and was ready to go. I straight away told her that would be nice, for her to finally go and see her babies. She had already declined though, said she wanted to wait for me to arrive so I could go with her. I grabbed the opportunity. "You go honey, I'm going to be another couple of hours, the girls are waiting for you, I will meet you on the ward". She was reluctant in her reply and said she'd see how she felt after breakfast. She had also started expressing milk the day before and wanted to try for more after getting off the phone with me. I didn't push it further and left her to it.

I once skydived. If you have ever jumped out of a plane, you will most likely have experienced the anticipation and

167

adrenalin that builds up on the short flight to reach the planned jump altitude. And as you sit at the open door of the plane with your legs hanging into the rushing air, thousands of feet from solid ground you realise that once you jump, either the parachute will open - or it won't. The drive to the hospital with Frank (my father in law) was bringing the same build-up of emotions the closer we got to our destination. Although I was not throwing myself out of an aeroplane that morning, I knew I was heading into a situation that had two possible outcomes, as does skydiving. One good, one not so good. Frank and I talked calmly on the drive. He's a man who doesn't rattle easily and as an ex naval military man he's a straight shooter. We talked about Stacey and raising girls. He has a lot of faith in his youngest daughter and sees the same strength in her that I do. The conversation brought a temporary distraction from the concern that was bubbling under the surface.

The traffic was light, so we arrived a little quicker than anticipated. I was anxious to get onto the recovery ward and see my wife. My heart started pumping a fraction faster as we entered the sliding doors of the maternity unit. We were buzzed through the second set of security doors and made a beeline for the ward that Stacey had been moved to. There was an expulsion of relief as we approached her bed to find she wasn't there, a nurse explained that she had been taken down to see the triplets over an hour ago. It seemed the hurdle she was facing the previous day had finally been overcome.

I was sensing hope as we walked the long corridor through the labour ward and into the quiet entrance of the NICU. I pressed the intercom and again introduced myself proudly as the Triplet Dad. The box immediately let out a shrill buzz and we walked through and turned the corner into the room that accommodated our daughters. I looked across the nurse station and right there, sat between Ava and Lacey's incubator was my wife, with Ava resting peacefully on her skin. She looked up on hearing us walk in and I was met with a beaming smile like I hadn't seen in a long time. The lights were back on in her eyes, the tension in her face was no longer there. She was wide awake and present. My tears were hard to hold back as I felt the sense of joy emanating from her as she held one of our tiny daughters. Every single fear that had taken a hold of her, all the anxiety she was struggling to contain since the day of that first scan had left her, the moment they placed Ava in her arms. In that moment I had no doubt in my mind that it was all going to be okay, that we as a family were going to be okay as the waves of tension and fear also left me. We now shared the same sense of purpose, the same sense of love. It was a beautiful moment that connected us back together after what seemed a long and difficult time apart. The nurses moved another chair next to Stacey and asked if I would like skin time with Ava so Stacey could hold Lacey.

Skin-to-skin time was an important opportunity for me to bond with my girls. For the babies to stay warm against me and to familiarise themselves to my scent and feel. I took my shirt off, got comfortable and Ava was carefully lifted among the tubes and wires and placed on my chest with a blanket placed over us. It was the first time I had held her for any length of time. She was tiny, her little face pressed against my chest as I supported her body against mine with one hand. I couldn't take my eyes off her. She was so perfect, so at peace in my presence. Lacey was taken carefully from her incubator and passed to Stacey to hold for the first time. We sat there each holding a baby, occasionally looking at each other in tears and laughing in joy at what we had achieved. I have never experienced such a peaceful sense of perfect connection to anything in my life. I wondered as I sat there if I would feel the same when I held the other two. Eventually Ava was placed back into her incubator and I was given Lacey, as little Blakely was brought out and untangled before being given to Stacey. The tears of joy didn't stop welling up in me as I held Lacey against me. My heart was exploding. It was partly in pure relief that we had made it.

Stacey explained she feared that when she saw her babies' she would feel nothing for them following the depression and dread she had experienced throughout her pregnancy.

It was why she was making excuses not to go and visit them the day before. She really did feel no connection to them and resented me for the connection I felt. She had become overwhelmed with the fears surrounding the whole experience, to the point that she later confessed to me that she was purposely mean to me in the hope that It would drive me away so that I would leave her, in which case she could terminate the pregnancy and not have to go through with it anymore. I wasn't angry when she told me this, nor did I judge her for feeling that way. If anything, it saddened me to hear the extent of her suffering. I know how it feels to be riddled with fear, unable to escape the constant thinking that feeds it. It's an easy problem to solve with the right meditation, the unique exercise I use had helped her overcome her panic attacks a couple of years previously, but she didn't want my help when she was in that place. I felt the stings of her anger and the tension of her anxieties but unless someone is ready for help, they will never accept it and to push it only makes it worse. When you're sat in the darkness, sometimes the light seems beyond reach. It had been that way for Stacey.

Blakely was the last of the trio I held. At 3lb 4oz she was still a good weight for the smallest of the triplets but to me she was like a miniature doll. Her skinny little arms and legs would make little involuntary movements when she laid in her incubator, she would twitch like she was dreaming in light sleep. Whereas the other two were still, Blakely seemed to have some activity going on in her. The day before, when first visiting them she would settle when I held her tiny hand with my fingers, place my other hand on her head and talk quietly to her. The nurse commented that I had a calming effect on her. I told the nurse about how much I had spoken to them while they were in Mum's tummy and she said that she would know and recognise my voice from those times. She was passed to me from Stacey careful as to not get tangled in the wires that streamed from the equipment next to us. I felt the same humbling sense of absolute connection and pure love. She was noticeably smaller than her sisters but with as much of a presence of spirit. I just sat there and stared at her tiny face, kissing her head and telling her all about the love she was going to know from her family now she was here.

The vows I had said to Frankie on the wedding day were ones I gave to my daughters that morning. I prayed as I held each one, for the strength and guidance to take care of them with the best of myself. It was one of the most memorable days of the whole experience, the calmness of that morning was perfect. The love we felt, infinite. There is something incredibly humbling in holding a new-born child for the first time. We are one of the only species on earth born in need of absolute care without which we would not survive. Maybe it's set up that way so we as human beings are given the chance to understand and know the love that comes from giving ourselves completely to someone else. Becoming a parent becomes the ultimate selfless act. The responsibility I felt was immense, though it didn't frighten me. I felt love for them and knew that connection would be enough to begin my journey with them.

The NICU is a place of calm. The nurses didn't only take care of the babies, they also took the time out to see that we as parents were doing okay. To make sure we were resting enough and coping ourselves. They were fully aware of the emotional strain we would have been under leading up to the birth. They made sure as Dad that I was fully involved from day one. They showed me how to wash and hold them. I was so careful when picking them up for the first times, they seemed so fragile and I was scared I may hurt them, but the truth was they were tough little cookies, as all babies are. It took me a while to get confident in handling them. I got the chance to change Ava's first poopy nappy, a skill I would soon master at expert level! The nurses took a real interest in my involvement and I jumped in feet first, doing as much as I could for our trio. If you have ever spent time with little ones in the NICU, or are expecting to spend time there, my advice would be to take that moment out of the storm to relax. To look after Mum and let the nurses take care of them as much as they can. They are the best carers in the world for the babies', so you have a golden opportunity to catch up on sleep in a stress-free environment. Trust me, those nurses are angels. The only pressure we experienced came from elsewhere in the family.

It had been promised to us at our local hospital that the triplets would be moved straight back there on the condition they were healthy without complications which they were, other than a slight bit of jaundice which is not uncommon with preemies. Stacey's Mum was keen right off the bat to get them moved, and understandably as she was taking care of most things at home. There was pressure on me to start making phone calls to our local hospital to get the ball rolling from day one, I had spoken with the head ward nurse, but it was never going to be that simple. And to be honest it was the last thing on my mind those first couple of days. The NICU nurses were aware of our situation. We were all aware of the situation. But we also had three babies in incubators who needed to gain strength and Stacey who was recovering from major surgery. As far as I was concerned the babies were exactly where they needed to be, my wife was calm and focused completely on the triplets and didn't need any more stress after the ride she had been on. All she cared about was being with her daughters on the ward. Nothing else mattered during those first few days. Yes, it was an inconvenience that we were in a different town, but in the scheme of things it wasn't a huge problem.

The evenings were the most enjoyable time for us, we didn't have to worry about visitors or any other distractions. It was us and the girls. Stacey had begun hand expressing small amounts of milk that we took each time to give to the babies. She had decided before they arrived that she wanted to breastfeed them. I was dubious as to if it was even possible to be able to produce that much milk, but the body is an amazing machine. Once stress was removed from Stacey her body was able to naturally work as nature intended. She didn't get worked up or worried when only tiny amounts came through to begin with, she just remained calm and persevered.

The babies preferred time to wake was in the middle of the night. On that second night I was switching between Ava and Lacey while Stacey had a moment with Little Blakely. She whispered me over to the incubator, smiling and telling me to look at Blakely as she held her fragile hand. As I looked in, I saw her laying on her back with her head turned to Stacey with her eyes wide open looking straight at us. I can't explain what I felt when I looked into those eyes, there was a deepness in them that pulled me in like a vacuum. It was like looking into a pure soul with an untouched heavenly connection, yet to be affected by the pressures and stresses of the world. It moved us both on another level. We captured that moment in a photo. Stacey always says that looking into her eyes that night made her believe in something bigger in the universe. I already have a faith; my wife was given her own experience that night. We shared a perfect day. There was nothing happening anywhere else in the world that was important. It was just us and the triplets, free from any distractions and immersed in the encompassing energy of love that exists, and always rises above when fear is no longer present.

Chapter 16

A little miracle

Early on the third morning I arrived back at the hospital to the news that Stacey was to be discharged that day. I was taken aback at how quickly she was deemed fit to go after experiencing such major surgery, but the head ward nurse felt she was okay to leave on the condition of plenty of rest.

The NICU has a corridor of adjoining rooms, which are reserved primarily for mothers with babies who have been moved to the unit from elsewhere in the county and have no means of travel. Stacey was kindly given a room. Not so much because of the distance but because she had triplets on the ward and was beginning to express milk for them. Unfortunately, the tiny room wasn't practical. We could not fit our baggage and all the needed equipment into it as well as ourselves. And the small single bed was far too small for Stacey to get comfortable in. Besides which, she was still in a lot of pain from the surgery and would struggle to get in and out of it from a lying position without help. I spoke with a ward nurse explaining our dilemma, she said she would get back to me but didn't think we had any other options.

Luck was on our side though. The nurse returned to us to

happily announce that a couple were leaving later that morning, and that a large room with a king size bed and furniture would be free for us to use for the duration of the triplets stay. It was good news for me too as it meant I could stay with Stacey and the triplets for a few nights while her Mum was at home taking care of Frankie for us. I also had the rest of that week off work so I would be able to spend some quality time with my wife and daughters while they recovered, and before I returned to the grindstone. By which time the triplets would have been moved to our local hospital which would make all our lives easier being that the hospital is five minutes down the road from our house.

We began another relaxing morning on the ward, spending skin time with the babies and with Stacey pumping to encourage the milk through. We had more excited visitors arrive later that morning. Around lunchtime, having moved all our belongings into the new room I was returning to the ward when a young Dr walking towards me, stopped and introduced himself. He asked if he could speak with Stacey and me in private regarding some important scan results. I told him we would be on the ward all day and he arranged to meet with us shortly. Walking back to give Stacey this news I felt rising concern.

There was obviously a problem. It wasn't worth guessing so we waited for him to arrive with more information. We both agreed before he arrived that whatever the problem, we would deal with it. We had both known the risks from the start. When he walked onto the ward, Stacey, her sister and I were sat among the incubators. He asked me if we were ready to go somewhere more private. Stacey said she wasn't moving and was happy for him to share any news where we were. He pulled up a stool and explained that the day before, the triplets had been given a routine brain scan, a typical procedure with new-born multiples and premature babies.

There was an issue with Blakely's results. My heart dropped in that second. He informed us that her results showed a bleed on the brain, a hemorrhage most likely caused by the trauma of her birth. As he talked another doctor was setting up some scan equipment next to Blakely's incubator. The plan was to get her booked in first thing the following morning for an MRI scan to find out the exact location of the bleed to determine the next move. A short scan was done as we sat talking with him and a piece of paper was handed to him by the technician. He held it up to us, it was a grainy photo of Little Blakely's brain, the scan was clear apart from a black shadow spreading outwards from the centre of what looked like the crown area. My heart kept sinking as I tried to process his words. Stacey took the news in but didn't allow herself to become overwhelmed. She had three babies to take care of and we would know more the following day. She kept herself calm and focused on the job at hand. We finished up talking to the Doc and I walked with him as he left the ward. I asked him what it could mean for her. He was honest with me. It could mean serious problems with mental development or motor skills, depending on which part of the brain was being affected, and depending on how quickly it could be treated. He told me there was a possibility she would be moved the following day to St Michaels hospital in Bristol for brain surgery.

He prepared me, and I thanked him. He left the ward and I took myself to the bathroom before going back to my wife. I locked the door and got hit with emotion as I tried to take in the information around my little girl. It was serious, and I was flattened by the thoughts going through my mind. I could deal with any outcome but losing her. I took a moment to get it out of my system then I splashed my face with cold water and composed myself. I needed to be on the ball. Emotionally for my wife and for the coming events. Knowing that the next day, we could now have two babies in Musgrove hospital and one in St Michaels undergoing surgery was a looming emotional and logistical nightmare, especially now Stacey was expressing milk. Blakely was struggling to digest formula and hold it down, breast milk was all she was able to tolerate, and she needed her strength. I would of course go to Bristol if need be while my wife took care of Ava and Lacey. Blakely would need a parent by her side. I got myself back to the present and made my way to the ward.

Stacey was calm when I returned. I didn't tell her about the possible moving of Blakely for surgery though, it was only a possibility and I didn't want to concern her while she was in the middle of trying to feed the babies. She had just come down from months of dread and anxiety and was calm and collected - I didn't want to rock that. As she said, "we have three babies here to take care of, so let's do that today". And she was right.

We carried on that day as normal and had the occasional talk about Blakely. The consensus was that she was here, and we would deal with whatever may arise. I was nervous under the surface though, it saddened me to know there was a problem and that she may be facing a tough ride. I spent a little more time with her that day. Talking to her and praying with her in my arms for the strength to take care of her no matter what. The day passed by and I stayed the night with Stacey, it was always hard to sleep with the sound of the breast-pump humming next to me with a low vibration. It was a sound I got used to very quickly. In my mind was Blakely and what may be ahead of us. My wife was still unaware of the possible seriousness of her situation, but she too had things her on her mind that night.

In the morning we were both awake early. Stacey expressed more milk as I headed across the hospital grounds to grab some coffee and breakfast to bring back. I was anxious to find out what was happening with Blakely. We were told that the MRI was booked, and that she would be taken across early that morning. It couldn't have come fast enough. She was lifted from her incubator and placed into a mobile unit to be taken across to the main hospital building. The mobile incubator was strapped to a bed and two hospital porters were charged with transporting her on the short journey. A nurse from the NICU joined us and I pushed Stacey in her wheelchair. It was Blakeley's first trip into the outside world. If only exposed to the bright sun while we crossed the road, she was out in the daylight for a moment. We were taken through the main entrance to the waiting room, where the procedure Blakely was about to have was explained to us. The temperature in the scan room was kept low so Blakely's tiny body needed to be well wrapped up. She was taken through. The NICU nurse stayed with Blakely as My wife and I waited outside. And waited......and waited...... Until one of the scan team came out and phoned a doctor who promptly arrived and went straight through to the scan room. Nothing was said to us, but I didn't think It was a good sign, to me it meant a second opinion. Shortly after her arrival the doctor who had told us about the scan results was also called and asked into the room.

We sat outside waiting and eventually they all appeared. Our Doctor told us we would be informed of the results within the hour. Blakely was brought out and transferred back into the incubator and we all headed back to the NICU. Stacey remained calm and focused on the babies while we waited for the results. I sat out in the little garden next to the ward and made a call to my friend to have a chat about the possible day we may be heading into. His advice was as always "stay conscious, stay present for them". Stellar advice. Again, there was no point worrying about events that were yet to - or may not happen.

As I joined my wife and her sister back on the ward, the doctor walked in with a bounce in his step and a smile on his face. I was a bit confused by his posture and stood up to greet him and hear any news. He got straight to the point "The MRI scan came back clear, she's fine. Whatever it was is no longer there, there's nothing to worry about". He seemed pleasantly shocked as he explained the results and my heart sped up with excitement and relief. I asked if he was sure, that nothing was somehow missed? But he again reaffirmed the results. Blakely was okay.

Later that day I spoke with a ward nurse about Blakely. She told me that she had heard on rare occurrences of premature babies with serious brain bleeds somehow resolving them by themselves but had never personally known it to happen in the time she had worked as a nurse.

I like to think Blakely was taken care of by the same light of grace that brought her to us. It was fantastic news that left us free to get back to focusing our full attention on taking care of the girls. Once again, we could breathe easy. Little Blakely continued to grow stronger and to this day shows no signs of any problems with her development. She is my little miracle, full of spirit and one tough cookie.

Chapter 17

Highs and lows

Looking at a satellite image of an Atlantic hurricane is to see a thick swirling mass of inescapable energy, and in the centre is the eye of that storm. It's a calm surrounded by chaos.

It's exactly where I felt I was in the NICU, in the calm of a storm I knew at some point I would be stepping back into it. Everything was changing again emotionally for my wife and me; her entire focus had shifted to the babies. She could see little else around her. There was pressure on me to push for moving the babies to our local hospital, but my wife just shut off from it. She was in her element and so was I. As I said before (and it's worth repeating) if you have little ones in the NICU make the most of it. No matter what the circumstances, the babies are in the best of care and it can be the perfect chance to rest up physically and emotionally. Make sure you seize that opportunity as it may be a long time before a break like that presents itself again.

A nurse stopped me for a chat at the end of the third day and asked how my wife was doing, I told her she was doing great. As far as I could see she was. The nurse however didn't think either of us were getting enough rest. Stacey was spending most of her time on the ward, either attached to the breast-pump or sat with the triplets and she wanted me by her side. It was understandable that she wanted me involved with everything and I was making sure I was doing my bit, but I was also getting tired from the broken sleep (Though the NICU was a breeze in that respect. I really had no idea what was coming). The nurse told me to keep an eye on her because soon she was going to crash. Stacey was on a high and what goes up - always comes back down. The ward nurses knew this and wanted me to be prepared for it.

There was one major concern that began to bite at me that week in the NICU. How I would cope with the tiredness? Up until the arrival of the babies I always knew I needed plenty of rest to function on a human level, or at least to get through the day without acting on the grating irritation I always felt when I was tired. In short, I need my sleep and always have. There's also the fact that my job is physical and dangerous and needs my full concentration. I cannot afford to make mistakes.

Later into the pregnancy I aired my concerns on a Triplet Dad group on a social media site. I asked how others managed tiredness with their work and home-life. My question was met with a blunt response that was backed up by almost everyone else who jumped in on the thread, it simply read "You'll sleep when you're dead". Once again honesty is always the best policy when a man's wavering in the wind, a jerk back to reality needs no sugar coating. There was no way around it. I knew Dads at work who were exhausted with just the one baby to deal with and I had three coming home. I would just have to do my best, I had faith that my meditation practice would help me stay consistent and out of resentment. In truth I was going to suffer badly, and as a result so were my relationships with others, my job and my sanity. Sleep deprivation is no joke.

The babies were born on the Monday, and by the Friday we were notified that the NICU staff were more than happy with the trio's progress, so much so that they were to be moved to the minimal care ward. It was a bright, naturally lit ward with open cots and crying babies, unlike the quiet of the NICU. It was fantastic news and a step closer to getting us all home. I began discussing the transportation of the babies that day with the head of the ward. The plan was to move them one at a time in the same day using the NEST team, a specialist unit working out of Bristol and covering the south west of England transporting new-born babies between hospitals using a modified ambulance and a specially trained crew. The plan sounds simple but transporting triplets was never going to be that easy. Before we could even consider transporting the girls, the local hospital would need to have enough beds on the Special care baby unit to accommodate all three. That means three available beds at the same time on a ward that only has nine cots to begin with. This was not a move that could be planned to the letter.

There were many factors that had to be taken into consideration. Babies were being born all the time at our local hospital, and the NEST team couldn't commit to us alone for three trips in one day. Our babies were all healthy for a start. There were emergencies that could arise that would take priority over our situation. As the facts came in about the difficulty of moving them so the agitation grew in the family members who wanted them moved ASAP. We were left to focus on the triplets and told we would be updated of any news regarding the move.

It was nice to have the girls out of the confines of the incubators and into the open cots. By the Saturday morning they had all been moved across. On that ward was a small side room in which our babies had been placed, three in a row. They had a room all to themselves. It was good to be out of the way of everyone and a chance for us to be with them all together. It was then we began colour coding them so as not to get them mixed up. Ava always had a blue vest, Blakely a pink one and Lacey in yellow.

After the early morning routine of washing and dressing the babies, Stacey headed back to our room to get ready for the day. I stayed and sat with my girls. A ward nurse poked her head through the door and asked if I minded her joining me. I invited her in, and she sat and asked me how I was doing. My immediate response was to begin telling her how my wife was getting on with it all, and how proud I was of her....... She stopped me and asked again "no, I meant how are 'You' doing in all of this". I was stumped, it was the first time a professional dealing with us as a couple and as a family had asked me that question. So, I began talking, and wound up emptying my heart out to her about the pressure and stress of the pregnancy, and my concerns about everything regarding my wellbeing and my families from here-on in. It was a cathartic experience, all the feelings and thoughts that I needed to get out of me left me lighter after that talk. and I will be forever grateful to that nurse for giving me her ear and her time, it was the only time I was given the opportunity to offload with someone who really knew what I was facing.

As predicted by the nurse the day before, Stacey began to crash. The wave she was riding smashed into the reef and broke up as the tiredness hit and her adrenalin levels dropped. As the day went on talk began of moving the babies, possibly the following day. It was welcome news for everyone, and we no longer had any reason to be in Musgrove hospital. Everyone was doing well. Stacey was on track in recovering and getting stronger by the day. Blakley and Lacey were both born with a little jaundice. It's not uncommon in preemies but the hospital wanted it cleared up before they could leave. So later that Saturday the twins were placed under UV lamps to treat them through their skin. There was a buzz again around getting the babies moved. Though for me and Stacey there was a little sadness that we would be leaving the ward.

Following on from such an intense start to the week we had finally regrouped as a couple at the hospital. It's as if at the first scan we split up and went separate ways, Stacey lost in fear and dread while I was filled with excitement. Both having entirely different experiences, yet side by side through it all. In the NICU we consciously met up again, and it was sad that soon it was going to all change. That ward became a quiet oasis and I knew the road ahead was going to be an arduous one as I adjusted to our new life. I began experiencing fear again, compounded by the tiredness that was now kicking in and the reality check I was getting punched with. I think we both would have been happy to have stayed there, at least a little while longer.

We got the call Sunday morning that it was possible to move one of the babies that day unless an emergency elsewhere arose. The other two would be transported the following morning. Our local hospital had a side room become available with a large open cot in which we could place all three babies, on the condition they were only attached to heart monitors and feeding tubes. A window had opened although it wasn't ideal as it would mean splitting them up from Mum who was providing the milk, but it was our best shot. If we passed it up it could mean a long wait before moving three in a day was going to be possible. We agreed to the move. My paid week off work was up, and I was due back in the following morning, so we organised for Ava to be moved that day. I would then drive over later that night with a supply of milk, enough to get her through the night and the following day until her sisters and Mum joined her. It meant I could drop in and see Ava at the hospital on my way to work. For me it was good timing, I wasn't going to lose any wage and the babies and Mum would be five minutes down the road. It was a rough day for Stacey, she had hit a wall of exhaustion and spent the day either in tears or asleep. She was understandably upset that Ava would be on her own over night, but it brought some comfort that I would be seeing her later that evening; and that they would all be reunited within the next 24 hours.

The NEST team arrived after lunch. To transport babies, they use a purpose-built pod. It looked like a blue torpedo strapped to a bed in which the baby is placed and secured. It all happened quickly, we had a bag packed with her clothes, blanket, nappies and little red teddy which was to go with her. She was carefully placed inside and moved out to the ambulance ready to go with a supply of milk to get her through until I arrived later that night. Di would be waiting for her at the other end so she wouldn't be alone, and she would stay with Ava while she settled. And as fast as they arrived, the NEST team left with Ava. All that was left was to wait to hear she had arrived safely and for Stacey to get back to expressing milk.

I could feel myself coming down from the adrenalin as well as Stacey that afternoon, though mostly I was just relieved that we had a plan in motion that would get us one step closer to home.

I had had a brief break from the emotional ride we had been on in the hospital. Those few days together with my wife and the triplets was a time I won't forget for many reasons. I was starting to get that feeling one gets running up to the end of a holiday, when your focus starts shifting to the reality of getting back to the grind rather than relaxing away from the distractions and monotony of life.

My last day in Musgrove was spent tending to the babies and keeping my wife comfortable and calm. Ava had enough milk to take her up to the midnight feed, so at 10pm I kissed the girls and my wife goodnight, said my goodbyes to the staff who had taken such loving care of my daughters and Stacey and left with milk packed on ice for Ava. It was a quick drive to our local hospital late at night with no traffic about. I pulled up outside the entrance to the women's unit, buzzed up to the Special baby unit that were expecting me and explained I had fresh milk for Ava and waited for the doors to open.

Ava was on the top floor and I made my way up without seeing another soul. I passed through another two sets of security doors and was met by the shift nurse. She took me to a side room and lying there fast asleep all swaddled up was my daughter. She looked odd in such a big cot on her own, but she also looked peaceful and it made me smile to see she was okay. The nurse said she was all fine and had settled well. She took the milk to store and I stayed for a while. I sat with my open hand on the back of her tiny head to comfort her with my warmth and told her all about the day and that she wouldn't be alone for long.

We enjoyed a calm hour together with nothing but the dim night lamp and the quiet beeping coming from the incubators on the ward at the end of the corridor. It was comforting to know that both Stacey and Frankie had begun their life on the same floor of the same hospital. I could easily have sat with her all night. I called Stacey to let her know all was well and made my way back home. I was out as soon as my head hit the pillow in the comfort that all was well with the world that night. I felt good that Ava was only a stone throw away if she needed me.

Chapter 18

Reunited

My morning routine hasn't changed since the day I got sober. I wake up, do my business and make a cup of tea. Then I say a short prayer and meditate for about fifteen minutes. The meditation I practice is a powerful awakening exercise, that allows me to pull back from my thoughts and observe them neutrally. It's the difference between walking out the door mentally prepared for the day with clarity or stumbling out the door carrying the stresses brought on by the overthinking that's ready to start kicking my ass as soon as I open my eyes.

In that sense, I am either awake 'conscious and present' or asleep 'unconscious and lost in thoughts'. The conscious state the exercise brings me to has allowed me to deal with the ups and downs of life without fear and doubt overwhelming me. Instead I have been able to make clear decisions based on natural intuition, rather than trusting my forever doubtful, over thinking mind. It doesn't mean I don't experience waves of negative emotions occasionally; I just don't get affected by their pull as I once did.

I got to the hospital early Monday morning which gave me a

194

good hour with Ava before I left for work. I called Stacey from the hospital, and she was looking forward to getting the babies back together. It felt strange returning to work so quickly after the birth, but I couldn't afford to take paternity leave. I needed to earn to pay the bills. I was met with congratulations and handshakes from the men I work with. As I walked into the workshop my phone rang, it was Stacey and she sounded distressed. "They're not moving them today"! She was shaking in her voice as she talked. There had been an emergency that took priority with the NEST team and they couldn't tell us when the transportation window would be available. It could be days or longer. It was a rough position to be in. Stacey stuck in Taunton with the twins, Ava in our local hospital without a milk supply while I was stuck back at work. Stacey's Mum was as upset as she was by the new turn of events.

I told her I'd call her back in five, I needed a moment to think. I was pissed off that the well-oiled engine of a plan was now seizing up and grinding to a halt. A supervisor from another department noticed my agitation, he walked over and asked what was up. After I explained to him about the spanner that had been jammed in the works he passed on some welcome news. He told me that at the end of the previous week's supervisors and managers meeting the owner of the company had walked in halfway through to announce, "that man who's just had the triplets – do everything you can to help him out". I was told to go, sort it out and not to worry about work.

I had been thrown a lifeline and I was able to leave without the added stress of worrying about my job. I shot out the door, sat in the car and came up with a plan before I called my wife. I figured the best thing for me was to get to Musgrove while Di stayed with Ava. It also meant I could bring milk back later that afternoon. There was going to be a lot of back and forth trips for me and Stacey's Mum but together we could manage it as well as fitting in the school run with Frankie. I raced home and got changed, stopped at the supermarket to grab supplies for Stacey and made my way back to Musgrove. When considering what some parents go through, our circumstances at that time were a minor blip. None the less, it was stressing my wife and mother in law out, so I needed to stay calm. If Stacey got too wound up it could affect her milk supply, and this would be the worst time for it to slow down.

When I arrived at the hospital I checked in with Stacey before heading down to speak to the Nurses on the ward. She was full of agitation and frustration, the opposite of where she needed to be for the babies and herself. I didn't let myself get pulled into the negativity that was present in the air, I knew what was happening and getting upset would serve no-one. She offloaded to me how she felt, and I hoped a vent would open the valves a bit and let some steam out the boiler. The pressure was again being pushed back on me to sort it, even though it was out of my hands. The nurses told us that we were back to the starting point of waiting for a window to move our other two babies. The next couple of days were tense. I ran back and forth with milk for Ava as did Di. Between us and Stacey's sister we were able to stick with the school runs for Frankie, spend time with Ava, and be with Stacey and the babies. I stayed overnight with my wife.

On the Tuesday morning we were met with another problem. The NEST team were available, but Stacey's Mum had called to inform us that our local hospital had had two newborns arrive over-night. Space wasn't an issue as we had the large cot ready. The problem now was that there were not enough staff available to look after all the triplets. My wife was clearly aggravated. She decided she wanted to go over, to see Ava and to speak to the staff and our consultant. The twins had enough milk pumped for us to leave for a few hours, so we left them in the good hands of the NICU staff and made our way over to our hometown.

It was Stacey's first trip out of the hospital, and she was back on the war path! I had seen a new side to my wife when she was pregnant, as did a few other folks including our consultant when the boat was rocked. I almost felt sorry for the staff that would be meeting us at the other end. They may have been doing their best but as far as my wife was concerned, they need to start doing a hell of a lot better. And Stacey would have no problem and absolutely no filter when explaining her grievances.

We buzzed onto the ward and headed into Ava's room. A staff nurse came in and introduced herself and told us that our consultant and the staff had just had a meeting and arranged to get more staff in. The problem it seemed had been solved, and the babies could be moved the following morning. I was relieved - mostly for the staff nurse that was passing on the news! She had no idea about the grilling she had avoided that morning. We had a good few hours with Ava giving Stacey a chance to familiarise herself with the ward and to speak with some of the staff taking care of our little one. The whole move now rested on the availability of the NEST team. Unless a prioritising emergency cropped up the babies would finally be cuddled up together for the first time on the outside. And we would be home, getting ready for the next chapter.

Early Wednesday morning we were sat up in bed, the breast pump humming and the heat of the sun already warming the room. My phone began ringing and I grabbed it presuming it would be Di waiting on any developments. It was a number I didn't recognise and the voice on the end brought some welcomed news. It was a man who worked for the NEST team. He went on to explain that they had a new travel pod, designed to transport two babies at once. It had never been used in the field so to speak, so Lacey and Blakely would be the first babies in the country to be transported using it if we were happy for them to go ahead. I had no issues with that plan. He also asked if we could have a few photos taken for publicity and a story that was to be published.

Stacey could see by my reaction on the phone it was positive news. When I relayed the conversation, she was excited and relieved. The team were coming in within the next couple of hours, so we needed to get moving and packed up. I made a few calls to the family, passed on the good news and once again all was well. Stacey's agitation left and her mood lifted. Blakely and Lacey were both well and ready to go and while my wife tended to the girls, I packed up the room and loaded the car with a lot more luggage than we had arrived with. It became apparent just from packing up at the hospital that we were going to need a bigger car - it was already full to the brim without even one baby in it!

We were sat waiting in our little side room when the ambulance arrived outside the ward entrance. Two women came through with the double pod strapped to a bed. They wasted no time in placing the babies in with their blankets, securing them for the hour-long journey which they told us they would be making a lot quicker than we would with blue lights. We both got a little emotional leaving the ward and saying our goodbyes. The professionalism of the NICU nurses and staff was exceptional. The NHS may have its problems, but our experience in Musgrove hospital was made all the easier by the care of the staff, they went out of their way for us. The babies were taken care of by angels in their first days. Leaving was exiting but also brought apprehension. We were heading once again into a new environment and a new situation.

Everything that tempted me to worry was outweighed by the fact we had three healthy babies who would be reunited within the next couple of hours. The NEST team beat us to our district hospital and when we arrived on the SCBU they had already placed Lacey and Blakely in the cot with Ava all neatly swaddled up. It was a beautiful sight to see them all tucked up together for the first time. The team left them with a little certificate each for a keep sake. It was quite an honour for them to be the first babies to be transported that way. For us it was a massive relief, especially for Stacey. She was free to visit any time she wanted to and could also get back to some much-needed home comforts and Frankie at night. The plan was to keep the triplets in the routine they were already introduced to, so that when they eventually came home, we had some structure in place for them, and for us. It was now just a case of all three fully feeding from the breast and we were free to go. They had all latched by the time we'd moved them, so it wasn't going to be too long before they were off feeding tubes and coming home.

For me it was back to work on the Thursday, while Stacey and Di spent their days with the triplets. I planned to see them each morning and take milk in before work. It became my quiet bonding time and those moments became so important to my coming mental health. Each time I spent alone with them was a chance for me to connect with them. To see the bigger picture of what my purpose was. I'm glad I put that effort in because I was walking into a turbulent time. My wife had suffered through the pregnancy but was now falling into her natural role. After the excitement of the pregnancy, I was about to start slipping into depression. The number one cause was resentment. And the instigator of all my coming problems? Sleep deprivation - for any parent it's inescapable, and it sucks!

Chapter 19

Hitting home

Looking back, those early days were a breeze. While the babies were in hospital we could come and go as we pleased, sleep at home and get rest. On an emotional level I was beginning to hit a wall. There was tension between myself and my Mother in law and most of that tension was coming from me. The problem (in my head) was that I was starting to feel edged out. As I went back to work, Stacey and her Mum took care of the babies during the day. There was no way around my position as we needed money coming in. But all I could see was that her Mum was stepping in to take over from me.

For generations there were families in which the men worked and didn't have a great deal of involvement with their babies. Mum's dealt with that whole side of it. Sometimes there is the left-over presumption that in fact, men have no real sense of what they're doing when it comes to babies so therefore are best out of the way. I sensed (in my already tired and aggravated sate) this opinion from my Mother-in -law.

The truth was she came to help us both out as she promised

202

she would. Not only that but she had moved in so I could go back to work and keep the wolf from the door. She was there for both of us, but my fear of being shut out was very real and being compounded by tiredness - all I began to see was a threat. I know parents of multiples that have separated and divorced because the help from in-laws became perceived as unwanted interference. Men are up against it when a baby arrives to stay out of the self-pity trap and step up to the table, no matter what's happening around them. My duty was to the babies and I was on a mission to prove that I wasn't going to be a deadbeat Dad avoiding any of my responsibilities. Unfortunately, I was also tired and paranoid which was making everyone's life hell.

We didn't sail into the pregnancy in a good place in our relationship. It had been getting to a point where a line had to be drawn; we couldn't carry on in unhappiness. I then had to deal with Stacey struggling like she never had before during the months of the pregnancy. The tension and her aggravation towards me only got worse. We finally reconnected in the NICU with the safe arrival of the babies. For a fleeting moment we were on the same page after all the stress of the pregnancy. I felt our relationship was beginning to finally get back on track. And now all her focus had shifted solely on to the babies.

The fear rising in me was that the disconnection she felt

towards me before and during the pregnancy was still present. What if she was still unhappy in our marriage? What would happen to us now? I could never talk to her about my concerns about us during or immediately after the birth as she was too distracted to listen to anything I had to say. It hit me once the dust had settled with the babies being moved to our district hospital that I still may not be the man she wanted in her life. If you erased the events of the last seven months, were we still two people unhappy in a marriage? This thought kept piercing my mind which only drove my feelings of paranoia. I truly believed I was being edged out under my own roof.

My resentment only got deeper the day the babies had their birth certificates registered. There were changes made to the triplet's middle names without my consent and it was passed off to me as no big deal. I hit the roof. In my head I was already feeling pushed out and now my wife and Di were making decisions about my daughters as if my opinions and wishes were not important. It was a massive disrespect to me as their father and I was damned if my daughters were going to grow up in an environment where a father's opinions are less than mother's and that it's okay to disrespect them. Especially the man who is working to provide for them and raise them.

It caused a horrible argument around the babies on the

ward, but I wasn't budging. I made it very clear that from there on in any decisions at all affecting our children were made with both of us, or not at all. And the anger that got into me that day festered under the surface as I comfortably entertained thoughts of bitterness and judgment. Although I kept a lid on it for the most, everybody felt on eggshells around me. The tension caused by that argument culminated in my wife snapping a few days later. She stormed off the ward and left me with the babies and had no intention of returning until the atmosphere I was creating dissolved. The result was that I had to drop any animosity I was carrying for the sake of peace at home. Stacey's exact words to me - "You need to sort your shit out or this is going to be a nightmare". Harsh but once again right.

I had to let go of my resentment.

But when tired and stressed the attachment to negative thinking is a like an adhesive bond, that without the light of consciousness is impossible to unglue. There are people on this planet, such as my wife, who can move on from an argument immediately from the point of resolution. There was a time that it baffled me how these folks performed such miraculous feats of forgiveness. I on the other hand, being an ex-problem drinker with anger problems lived with the kind of ego that wouldn't let go of any incidence that caused me upset - especially when my prideful spirit got dented. I can unconsciously get lost in fantasy arguments in my head with someone who pissed me off by looking at me the wrong way thirty years ago. Pride is an ugly thing.

The meditation I practice had solved the resentment and over thinking problem I once had. But that ability to stay free from anger/fear in the stream of life is contingent on staying conscious 24/7. It takes a daily commitment to meditate and a vigilance to watching for negative thoughts. And my practice was already beginning to fall by the wayside. Little agitations were biting without a defense against them. As a friend elegantly, puts it "without the light of conscious awareness you're walking around with your pants down". And I was, and I didn't even see it happening. All I could see was that others were causing me problems. In my head I was under attack! in truth I was just becoming self-absorbed with my resentments.

*

Unbeknown to me, premature babies sleep a lot. It's normal. As far as their hormones are concerned, they are still in Mum's tummy developing in preparation for the big day. This lulled me into an almost foolish false sense of security. They slept, woke up and fed, didn't cry and after a cuddle went back to sleep. I would talk to the very suspicious guys at work about our new babies and their quiet routine, suggesting that perhaps my fears about screaming babies all day and night was not going to materialize. I mean if this was how they were going to be from here on in, it was going to be a sweet deal for me as far as adjusting to our new life went. Yes, we would have to get up to do the night feeds but in between we could rest and enjoy our new babies. Stacey's Mum perhaps wouldn't need to stay with us for as long as we first thought. Maybe having triplets was going to be easy-peasy!

This little 'soon to be smashed' fantasy I entertained kept me in good spirits during the babies last days in hospital. All the tests for their hearing and responses came back fine, they continued to gain weight and strengthen. Another routine brain scan did show a small shadow on Blakely's brain but there was no concern about it as she was doing as well in every respect as her sisters. The morning milk runs continued and I kept my routine of visiting them before work. At home it was all go with the preparation. The babies would be sleeping in our little bedroom with us to begin with. We had two cots placed at the end of our bed and a Moses basket on a rocking stand on Stacey's side of the bed. Having them in the room was going to make it easier to do the night feeds and we could keep a close eye on them. In the living room we had a large travel cot in which they could sleep during the day. Baths would be done on the kitchen table in a plastic baby bath to save us running up and down the stairs. And as Stacey was breastfeeding, we wouldn't need to stock up on formula or bottling equipment. The one thing that was plentiful in the spare room was nappies. When we knew we had triplets coming I contacted a lot of companies to see if they could offer us any freebies. Unfortunately for us they no longer hand them out due to the volume of multiple babies now conceived through IVF. I emailed pram and stroller companies too. Just on the off chance of any help. I felt It was worth a shot. Our finances were already taking a hit. But for the time being we had everything we needed to get by. It was just a case now of getting them home to begin their life with us.

All in all, the triplets spent twenty days in hospital. Nine days in Musgrove and eleven days in our local SCBU. I know parents who have little ones in for months before they are discharged due to complications. We were incredibly lucky that it all happened in a relatively quick time frame. Our triplets had become quite a presence on the ward. There were bank nurses asking for the night shift just to look after them. They were taken care of with absolute love and careful attention. It wasn't long after we arrived on the ward that the nurses stepped right back from making decisions around the triplet's care and feeding routines. Stacey was on the ball from the start. I can only imagine how daunting it must be for a new Mum to find her intuition in dealing with a new-born amongst the stress surrounding a birth. Yet Stacey, although not a new Mum, was shining with a natural confidence around the babies. She knew exactly what they needed and when.

It put a confidence in me to see her so switched on with our daughters. The nurses took their orders from Stacey. I thought they may have been a bit put out of joint by Stacey's forwardness in instructing them but on the contrary, they were impressed with her dealing with the situation as well as she was. At the end of the day those nurses wouldn't be there, and it would be my wife running the show at home. I thank God for Stacey's instinct as a parent. At least one of us knew what to do with three newborns. Being a new experience for me, my part was simply to follow her lead, take her instructions and support her decisions with them. If you're a new Dad unsure what to do at times - just ask, because there is always something to do.

The only way you can really become a spare part is if you let it happen.

Chapter 20

Zombie

Sleep deprivation is a horrible form of torture. The victim is kept awake in various stressful ways while their mind and body suffer from the torment. Without escape insanity is reached fast unless the mind and body are free to power down and revitalize. Welcome to parenting!

I began to suffer, if only a little in the early days before they even came home. But it was enough for me to become affected. My daily routine of meditation and rest was being disrupted and there was no avoiding it. I was just going to have to batten down the hatches and get on with my duties the best I could.

The triplets had finished all their routine check-ups and the nurses were confident in Stacey's decision to bring them home. They had all latched and were feeding from the breast so there was no need for them to be taking up precious space on the SCBU. The day they came home I was at work, so it was Stacey and Di who brought them back from the hospital. When I walked through the front door, I could see the cot in the living room through the hallway. The triplets were fast asleep. All swaddled up and peaceful in our home. There was

210

relief from both Stacey and Di and Frankie was also excited to finally have her sister's home. We had made the decision before they arrived that a strict routine had to be implemented and stuck to. We were already halfway there as they had accustomed to a structure of feeds and awake time in the hospital. It was now just a case of keeping it going at home. Everything was done to the watch with military precision. Babies need routine.

For the first few weeks Stacey took care of the night feeds which allowed me to sleep through. She and her Mum would take care of the midnight feeds. I was involved as much I could be when home, before and after work. Then one night, Stacey dozed off with a feeding baby on her which is dangerous. We talked the next day and the only safe conclusion was for me to get up with her for the duration of the feeds to keep her awake. It was then I felt the full brunt of sleep deprivation. From their last feed at midnight their next would be between 2 – 3 a.m. Each baby took around 20 – 30 minutes to feed, so by the time I got back to sleep (which wasn't always easy after being wide awake) I would get about an hour and a half of broken sleep before my alarm went off work at 6am. For a while I was able to get a nap in during the evening to make up for the lost sleep later in the night, but Stacey soon resented that I was getting extra sleep. And so, began the tit for tat arguments. If I mentioned I had to work and needed that couple of hours in the evening while the babies were napping and she was pumping, it was taken as the insinuation by Stacey that she wasn't working, I was simply trying to point out that my job is physical and dangerous without concentration. But as in the pregnancy my wife didn't want to hear it, and neither did her Mum. If Stacey wasn't resting, then neither was I! I would get told I didn't know how easy I had it, which just wound me up more. And she was right, we had an extra pair of hands in the house helping us out, but I was tired and aggravated and counting my blessings was the furthest thing from my mind.

Until then I had also been sleeping on the sofa at night and that first night back in my room was such a wake-up call. I'm a light sleeper. I need the room pitch black with zero noise, and I was now waking up with every little sound the babies made, unlike my wife who would have most likely slept through The Blitz. And that became another reason for me to get annoyed. I was constantly reminded from that night of the comment a triplet Dad once gave me "you'll sleep when you're dead".

It was a tough adjustment and we were all tired and feeling the strain. It was still a blessing that they went back to sleep straight after the feeds, but that wouldn't last for long. Had the babies gone full term their due date would have been the 19th of August. And just around that date it all stepped up a gear. The babies realized they were out - and awake suddenly meant awake! They found their lungs and knew how to use them. My little fantasy of the perfect sleeping quiet babies was well and truly hurled out of the window as I came crashing down to earth. It also became more difficult to get them back off to sleep. I would be stretched out across the bedroom floor, rocking Lacey's cot with one foot, my hand rocking Ava's cot while Stacey saw to Blakely. All exhausted and in need of rest.

I soon entered the twilight zone of tiredness, where the head constantly hums with a low-level vibration. I was functioning but not much else. I would drive to work in the mornings with the window wound down, my head stuck half out so the cold morning air would keep me awake enough to safely drive. At work I drank black coffee all day and went through the motions, I was there but not consciously present. I began making small mistakes on the job and turning up late. I could literally sleep standing up.

It was around that time I became familiar with the term 'witching hour'. Each night I would walk through the door to screaming babies. From around 4pm until their next feed they were grumpy, tired and hungry. Although I was feeling the stress I never got agitated with the triplets. They were only doing what babies do when brand new to the world, their little hormones firing off as they continued to develop. It was when I came home that I would take over trying to

213

pacify them.

Stacey and Di had been dealing with them all day, so it was my turn to give them both a break. I would cuddle one and rock two of the baby chairs with each foot as they screamed in unison. About two months after we got them home a decision was made to give them their last feed of the day in a bottle. It happened that way because Stacey had a cut on her nipple and so one day pumped the entire day to express enough for a bottle feed that night. It meant they would all feed at the same time after a bath and would then go down to sleep together. It also gave my wife a break. She suffered painfully occasionally from soreness with the feeds but would bite her lip as they latched and soldiered on. She loved feeding them, the closeness with them and the bonding. The decision to give them a bottle gave me an opportunity to get involved. And I absolutely loved feeding them. To see those little eyes staring at me over the bottom of the bottle was such a profound experience. I got why Stacey loved feeding them so much. As much as I struggled there were islands in the day; little moments of calm and grace with the triplets that kept my feet on the ground. I loved playing them music too. Bath times were always to the tunes of the Beatles. Abbey Road became a favorite. Playing the babies music was my way of connecting with them, sharing a part of myself with them in a way.

One weekend Stacey's Mum went home for a break. We had managed to get a cheap seven-seater car so decided we would take them out for our first trip. Westbay is a little fishing village about forty-five minutes from us. We figured it was far enough to get away from the house for a few hours, but close enough to get back if any disasters struck. Due to problems getting the prams delivered we only had a single, but the babies were so small all three fit in it perfectly. My first time out with the babies was a bit stressful. They had all pooped-on arrival, so we found a little café with a toilet which turned out to be too small to change them in. Stacey had no problem in changing them on her lap where we sat at the table. I felt a bit embarrassed and conscious of the other diners, I thought it a bit disrespectful to the onlookers enjoying their cream teas and Stacey felt my agitation and embarrassment. "Look Si, the babies need changing so we change them". I'd like to point out that I have no problem anymore changing a baby wherever we are, no matter who's about. That self-consciousness had to go. I also sing to them in public, make silly noises at them and couldn't care less of what others think. What counts is my babies are comfortable and happy. Besides which they pick up on stress, so if I'm feeling twitchy - they get twitchy. I have spent hours as a musician searching for deep meaningful lyrics to put to my music. Now from thin air I can burst into song, rock opera style about stinky bums and smelly feet without even trying. They are truly inspirational little beings.

Taking them out was also the introduction to other people's fascination and sometimes unwanted and unfiltered comments that would come our way. Until having my girls I had never came across triplets. They bring quite a crowd when they get spotted. Most comments are kind, especially from older people, we've had old ladies cry a tear of joy when they've stopped to see them. I am touched and understand their response. Some folks though are without any sense. One woman told my wife that if she found out she was having triplets she'd kill herself. I had a woman approached me while I was out alone with them to tell me the sight was enough to 'make her ovaries explode'! for once I was lost for words. These events are unavoidable. As is the interest. Some comments are very personal. I've been asked more than once how they were conceived, meaning 'are they IVF'. My stock answer is "well, when a man loves a woman very much and they want to make a baby, he puts his........." (I'm sure you know the rest). We do draw the line at photos though, and people touching them. Germs are one thing we don't want. Imagine dealing with three sick babies - we work hard to keep healthy. At the end of the day we have something very special that bring a lot of joy to others, they will always bring attention.

Going out with babies, as I discovered that day, is not like going out as before. We are constantly watching them and tending to them, planning the next step. Going out took real organizing, especially that first trip. All-in-all though, it was an experience we would have to get used to. But it was good to get away from the house. It was getting to be quite a claustrophobic environment.

I found my little bit of peace and solitude though, in the bathtub, I would light a candle, play some good music and relax for half an hour or try and meditate without falling asleep which was the problem I now faced with my practice. In the mornings I would try to be still for ten minutes before I left for work, and the moment I closed my eyes I would drift off. I would try again at lunchbreak in the car, but again I would just fall asleep. It was getting increasingly harder to stay conscious of my fears and agitations. I knew If I could keep meditating daily, I would eventually be released from the negative emotions that kept arising in me. I was also aware that I may have to struggle through until It was possible again. My saving grace was that I knew it was there and available. It was the solution to my resentment problem and I just needed to try and practice some patience and tolerance at home.

The days and nights began to blur into each other over the following weeks. I was constantly taking photos of the babies on my phone to look at during the day, so when I felt the sting of bitterness that was rising around our situation, I could remind myself of the bigger picture. Some nights I would drive home from work still exhausted from the previous nights. I would pull up outside the house and get hit with that feeling of deflation, knowing that when I walked through the door the babies would be screaming, my wife and Di would be tired from the day, and that I would be taking over. I would slump with my head on the wheel, take a deep breath and pull myself together. Self-pity is an ugly thing and I had to be aware of it pulling at me, and it did - daily. It's a case of doing whatever gets you through. The enormity of having three babies come home brings with it a massive weight of emotions. Trying to deal with those feelings without rest and sleep is impossible, yet we got on with it because we had no choice. Some days I felt I was carried through. Other days my head would adjust to the exhaustion enough to feel numb, and in that mental place I felt no irritation and could just enjoy what we had. I dealt with the pregnancy well, my optimism and intuition kept me solid emotionally. But there was nothing anyone could say, or any type of preparation that could have got me ready for those first couple of months at home. They are just hard. Really fucking hard.

Chapter 21

Awakening

Our nightly routine of rocking the babies to sleep was just getting silly. One night my wife had a brainwave. She switched the T.V on, found a hoover noise playing on repeat on You Tube and played it to the babies who instantly quietened down and fell asleep. Babies are comforted by white noise because it reminds them of the sounds they were used to in the womb. For me, I had to now adjust to sleeping to the sound of a hoover blasting all night long. It worked most nights (some nights it didn't) but it was a move that brought us a pinch of relief.

We also tried introducing pacifiers, but they were an absolute nightmare. They worked while they were in, but at night they would constantly fall out. They drove me nuts, just as one would settle another would drop out, quickly followed by the sound of a crying baby. I was up and down like a yo-yo every five minutes popping them back in. The dummies found the bottom of the bin quickly. So, for a while we used vacuum noises and a light projector on the ceiling. One night (to be exact the babies were nine weeks and three days) we finished up the last feeds around eleven thirty and settled them to sleep. The next conscious moment my alarm was sounding out for me to get up for work. We both shot out of bed in a panic to check they were all okay. And they were. For the first time they had all slept through without waking for the three am feed. I can't begin to tell you how happy we felt that morning, literally dancing around the bedroom. I had six hours solid sleep before work, and It felt amazing, like a long black cloud had been lifted to let the sunshine through. Once again, I got a bit too excited in thinking that missing a feed would be a permanent occurrence now, but they are babies. And babies do what they want to do and change like the wind. Some nights they still woke but at least a couple of times a week we were both getting a decent rest. Enough to recharge the batteries and for me to meditate regularly again.

It was a breakthrough that felt to me like a lifeline. I was already feeling the encompassing darkness of depression cloaking me just from the inability to stay conscious. I know that grip too well. I felt as though I was sitting on a rollercoaster that I couldn't see the end of. Being beaten with tiredness and fear/resentment day in day out was pulling me under. My resentments boiled below the surface. I had started having paranoid thoughts that Stacey and her Mum were edging me out, so Stacey would be free to take the babies and live with her Mum to raise them without me. I felt I was being scrutinized and judged for every little mistake I made. There were two thoughts that kept me afloat at times.

1 – These babies are a gift.

2 – I cannot fail them as their Father.

There was no way I was going to let them grow up without me in their life. I had painful talks with my friend when my thinking overwhelmed me. I began working out how I would cope and be able to see them if they moved away. Of course, it was all in my head. My wife had no intention of leaving, but I didn't know that, and I couldn't talk to her. All I felt from her was distance. The babies were her only priority. I would have to wait and hope we were okay when the storm blew over at home.

The time I cherished the most in those first months was my time with the babies. I loved being with them, they reminded me every day that there was something bigger at play. It didn't matter if they were screaming or smiling, I never felt any bitterness towards them for my deteriorating mental state. I prayed daily that God would not let me lose sight of the purpose I had been given. And to stay out of self-pity for their sake. They overwhelmed me with love, a love that carried me through some of the harder of days. It was all for them, and worth every bit of struggle.

One evening, Stacey Di and Frankie left me alone with the babies to visit her sister for a couple of hours. She was anxious about leaving them, but I encouraged her to go and have a break. She needed to get away from the house and I needed some alone time with my daughters. That night I began classic album time with the triplets, a tradition that continues to this day when it's just me and the babies. We listened to Pink Floyd's 'Meddle' and some classic Led Zeppelin. They stayed chilled for the whole couple of hours Stacey was gone. I could relax without feeling like I was being watched and the babies picked up on that calm. Stacey called within the hour to check all was well, I told her not to rush back, to relax herself and enjoy some time away.

It was a perfect evening, one I desperately needed with them, and one I will never forget. They lifted my spirits back up just by their presence. I was never worried about being on my own with them or if I could cope alone. I have never experienced any fear around that responsibility. When Stacey got back, she sat down with her Mum and surprised me with a comment. She told me that It was good that she was able to leave me alone and trust me with the babies, that not many new Dad's would be willing to do that. Finally, I got a grain of recognition. I'm not one for patting myself on the back, nor am I the sort that needs constant validation to keep my esteem on a cozy level. But believe me when I say it felt good to hear in the head space I was struggling with. I needed to hear it more than anything feeling the way I was at that time. It was big compliment, one that was seconded by my mother in law. It was a little reinforcement that I was doing alright, and I was grateful for it.

The thing with triplets is that it doesn't really get easier. All that happened was that we adjusted to each new development as the babies changed. This adapting would now become a lifetime of permanent momentum for us as parents, especially in their formative years. We had an ever-changing home in those early months. I had to learn to deal with tiredness. Once I was back meditating though I was able to step back from my overactive, over thinking mind again. I got a clarity back that frankly I was struggling to manage without.

There was a specific event that really woke me up. Di had left, and we were finding our feet as a family. It was all I wanted for us, to start reconnecting and dealing with our children as a couple. A week later Stacey told me that her Mum was coming back again, to stay for a few days. I was livid. I drove to work so full of anger my head was boiling. A work colleague asked me what was up, I was about to go on a self-righteous rant when I was hit with a flash of consciousness. A light bulb moment. It was like I had stepped back from myself and was staring at an angry bitter man, absorbed with his resentments and self-pity. It was a nasty sight. And it was who I had become over the months since the arrival of the babies. The truth was my wife was struggling with the anxiety of dealing with them during the day and feared being on her own, and I didn't even see it. I was making it all about me. Through my clouded judgement I had missed what was going on in front of me. Stacey was understandably upset by my negativity and she had felt on edge about announcing that her Mum would be coming to help again.

What a horrible situation to put my wife in. She had four children to deal with at home - and then me, stropping like some self-entitled man child because I was struggling with my own fears, wanting things to suit me. It was a painful awakening. I was causing all the stress under our roof. Yes, I was concerned about our relationship, but those fears had to be squashed. I had lost my way and my faith in my family. There would be plenty of time to talk later down the line but for now, we were both dealing with a highly stressful situation that wasn't just affecting me. We needed Di. I needed Di to be there for us and the babies. I had even purposely made her feel uncomfortable at the house just to get my point across that I wasn't happy she was there. What a royal asshole I had been!

I felt deeply ashamed of myself and the way I was behaving. I messaged Stacey to apologize and asked if we could talk that night, so I could explain and make my amends. I didn't want to be the man causing hurt to others. When Di came back, I waited for an opportunity to talk with her. I took responsibility for making her feel the way I did. I told her that I had become overwhelmed and all the anger I felt had nothing to do with her and that I truly appreciated everything she was doing. I made a conscious effort from that day forward to bring some peace back to my house. We have had a brilliant relationship since, and I always welcome her visits. She is amazing with the babies and goes above and beyond what many others could manage with them. I have a great respect for her. Other than my wife and myself she is the only other person who can deal with all three of them alone. I will always owe her a debt of gratitude. My anger left me that day and life began to improve for all of us.

That awakening had opened the door for Stacey and me to start talking. It opened a line of communication that allowed us to be honest with each other without resentment, and fear of upsetting one another. She began to talk about the places she went mentally during the pregnancy. The truth was she didn't want to go through with it one bit. She was so overwhelmed with fear and anxiety that she shut down from everyone. Each morning when she awoke, a dread descended and hung over her like a black cloud. Her biggest fear was that something would go wrong and she would lose her life. That Frankie would then lose her other biological parent. She was convinced that I would not be able to cope and would walk out the door, abandoning her with three newborns.

Her fears stretched to the point that she was purposely horrible to me in the hope that It would end our relationship. Leaving her free to terminate all of them so she didn't have to go through with any of it. It's no wonder she felt no connection to them and resented that I did. It was an awful place for her to be in. All that fear left her the day she held Ava, I saw it go myself, but it was still difficult to hear.

I wasn't angry at her for the way she had been with me. When people are infected with fear, they lose their original identity as they react to the thinking that fear produces. They become someone else and think and behave in ways that make little sense to others and even themselves. I had just been through the same, until I saw for myself what had happened to me. She told me that she would have fleeting moments of consciousness where she would be filled with the sense that it was all going to be okay, only to quickly sink back into the whirlpool of negative thinking. It was like God was reaching in, letting her know there was light in the darkness. And a fast as that flicker of light came, it was snuffed back out by fear.

What became crystal clear was that the only way we could fail was if we let resentment and fear come between us. We had to both make a commitment to remain conscious. She already had all she needed to be a loving mother to the babies, and I had the intuition to guide me to do the right things as a father. It was never the triplets that caused our anxieties but the improperly met stress of the event. They were innocent in it all. When we put love back at the centre of our marriage, everything else fell back into place. Yes, it was going to be a difficult road ahead, but if we were to raise the triplets in a loving environment we had to work together as a couple, with as little friction generating between us as possible. Honesty and patience with each other and ourselves had to be the ingredients for a home we could all thrive in. It was an ideal to grow towards going forward.

Chapter 22

Autumn

Autumn is my favourite time of year. The last burst colours of the dying leaves, the darker nights that roll in and the crisper cool mornings. I've always found comfort in change, maybe it's down to the momentum of moving that's always been present my life. In the past I rarely stayed still or in one place for long.

In the triplets first year came a time of big change for us too, as Stacey's Mum left after three turbulent months of helping us out. It was a hard adjustment for Stacey to deal with, just her and them on her own while I was at work. She had only a couple of visitors and the offers of help disappeared. It seems a common occurrence with multiple parents, as we discovered from meeting other Mums and Dads of high order multiples. My Mum's mobility isn't great, but she helped where she could. Mostly with Frankie's school runs in the afternoons. Most nights I would walk in and Stacey would be sat at the bottom of the stairs waiting for me to get back to take over. She would be exhausted. I used to send her upstairs to chill for a couple of hours while I pacified them. Occasionally I would bathe and feed them with a little help from Frankie, just to give her a night off. On a Friday I finish work early, so would take over as soon as I got home. And on the weekend, I would take them out on my own. Just a walk to the supermarket then to a local café. It gave Stacey and Frankie some time out to keep their relationship tended to.

We were both exhausted beyond words but there was one day, that I found a new appreciation for what my wife was dealing with while I was at work. During a weekend visit from Di, I had booked Stacey into a spa for the day. Her Mum came down to join her. I decided to have the triplets for the entire day. There was enough milk expressed to cover all the feeds. Unfortunately, Frankie was unwell that Saturday and had to spend the day in bed. So full of confidence and as mentally prepared as I could be, I was flying solo with them.

My day began at five thirty with the changing and feeds. Stacey left around ten, by which point the babies were already getting grumpy. As the day went on my stress levels were tested as I struggled to pacify them. When all three are screaming and tired they are quite a force! By mid-afternoon my head was banging, I would get one asleep in my arms but still be rocking two with my feet in their chairs, both screaming. It was intense. Stacey and her Mum stayed out for the whole day on my orders, enjoying spa treatments while I was clinging to my sanity, praying for the hours to go by until bath and bedtime.

Moments after I had bathed bottled and put them down to sleep, in strolled my wife, a big smile on her face looking as relaxed as a woman could be after a day's pampering. And here was me, thumping headache, eyes twitching with sudden onset madness unable to string a coherent sentence together. It was insane, I was shattered!

I never once thought my wife had it easy, however that Saturday gave me a new appreciation and respect for what she faced each day. My day job is physically demanding. Yet taking care of three babies is both mentally and physically draining. There's no opportunity to switch off, they demand constant attention and care. I think all working Dads should have a go at flying solo for the day when their babies are young, just to understand and experience what it is to be a full time stay at home parent to them.

There was another thing to look forward to that autumn, a celebration coming by way of the girls Christening. A tradition within Stacey's family. It was an opportunity for friends and relatives to get together and celebrate. To me it meant a lot more than that. Although I'm not a religious man and was never raised in a church community, in recovering from alcoholism I had my own experiences which led me to a personal faith. It was that same faith in the light of consciousness that got me through the pregnancy and kept me out of fear so I could be present for my family. And it had continued to guide me through the tougher times we were experiencing.

To many of us, the triplets were a miracle. A gift from God. The Christening, as I saw it, was a celebration of light. And the triplets shone brightly in all our lives. The godparents had been chosen months before. Stacey's two sisters along with their husbands and her nephew. And on my side, I chose my closest friend Paddy and his wife Linda to also honour that role.

Paddy and his wife live in London and we have only met in person once before. They arrived the previous day for a chance to see the girls on their own before the masses of Stacey's family arrived. As they walked into the living room to three sleeping babies, they were taken back. The triplets have a powerful effect on people, and they did with my friends. When they awoke, they were calm and curious about their visitors. Paddy and Linda had a chance to hold them and cuddle with them. And to my surprise the babies never made a sound. I know they can sense tension and they relax around people who are absent of it.

It was a peaceful couple of hours, catching up and sharing in the joy of our three remarkable blessings. I owe a lot to my friend. Although he never advises me on personal matters, he has been present through my entire sober life. A man with his feet on the ground who has helped anchor me back down during the times I have wavered with his honesty and ability to see past the drama to the bigger picture. There was no one else I would have asked to be a godparent to my girls.

The Christening was a special day. A break from the daily routine and a chance for those closest to us to meet Ava, Blakely and Lacey. And most importantly, to have them blessed at the start of their journey in life.

As we stepped into November our home life continued at a relentless pace. There was also a big sister adjusting to a hectic new life at home. Frankie, from day one, fell in love with her little sisters. But she too had her own struggles to face. She did everything she could to be helpful, from bottle feeding to helping me with the baths. She was confident with them - a little over-confident at times! - but she was learning the same as me. She was under no obligation to help and we had made that very clear from the start. To sit in a room with three fired up babies can grate on your nerves at times, so if she was ever feeling overwhelmed with the chaos downstairs, she would disappear to her room for a break.

I know the hardest thing for her was the tension resulting from the tiredness between Stacey and myself. It's incredibly difficult to be patient when exhausted. Before the triplets came along, we had all the time in the world for

Frankie, but that all changed overnight. We began to see little changes in her personality. Children under pressure, who cannot verbalise or make sense of how they feel, start to act out in various ways. Not because they are bad suddenly - but because they are experiencing conflict. She was picking up on our impatience, which in turn was adding to her insecurities. She began telling little lies. She would make up stories that she knew would get our attention. Spinning little yarns here and there that would shift our full focus from the babies to her momentarily.

We never punished her for it or resented her new behaviour because we could see what was happening. She was after all, a ten-year-old who had just been bombarded with three babies. And if we were feeling the pressure, Frankie was too. I made a point of talking to her and keeping a line of communication open. When a child sees impatience in parents without any explanation, they tend to soak it up, feeling as though they have done something wrong. Like they are the problem. And I made sure she understood that wasn't the case.

Frankie has a wise head on her shoulders, and she understood why there was occasional tension in Mum and me. She also knew it wasn't going to be forever, and that while the triplets were still babies, they needed our full care and attention.

It was after a few discussions that I showed her how to meditate on her request. She was dealing with stress the same as Stacey and me, and it was beginning to affect her at school and at home. I showed her how to observe negative emotions and thoughts when they popped into her head without getting lost in them, to be aware that they were there and not to resent or fear how she was feeling, or the situation she found herself in.

I had to show her a way to cope that was not reliant on Stacey, me, or anyone else for answers. A way she herself could begin to find her own natural intuition to cope mentally and emotionally in the middle of a highly stressful time. It wasn't long before she came back to being herself as her resentments and fears subsided. I have a huge respect for my eldest daughter and the way she has grown over the months. She has discovered some of her own independence along the way and remains Mama's little helper - and my shadow. She is a blessing to this family and will be a great role model to her three little sisters. And I have never felt any less love towards her than I do for the triplets. In my heart they all have an equal place.

During the couple of weeks following the Christening we found a certain rhythm at home. I had adjusted somewhat to the tiredness and the babies were settling nicely. I made the mistake again of getting comfortable in that groove. The problem with getting too cosy in a routine is that when it takes an abrupt turn it can throw you. Lacey came down with Bronchiolitis, a nasty chest infection that came on quickly. An afternoon at a fete at Frankie's school wound up with a trip to A&E. Blakely and Ava also came down with it. We were hurled back into sleep deprivation while taking care of three poorly chickens. With the chest infections came a taster of what was inevitably going to happen from time to time. Having three sick babies is no joke. There is good reason we are quick to stop strangers touching them when we are all out.

Sickness at home usually starts with Frankie, she brings all sorts back from school, but the winter of 2017/18 was particularly bad for chest infections and viruses in the UK. Whilst the babies were ill, I too came down with what started as a mild chest infection. Unfortunately, my body had no energy or down time to fight back due to tiredness and work. My immune system was running on empty. As the babies got better - I got worse. To the point I was in and out of A&E myself until one night I was admitted to hospital after a scan showed a dark spot in my left lung behind my heart. It was a hard time for me as the realisation that I couldn't afford to be ill sank in. As the doctors explained to me, the stress of the previous months had probably added to my poor health. I was burnt out. They suggested that I slow down a bit, which is easier said than done with triplets

235

and a desperately needed job to hold down.

Concerned about my health I was once again dragged back into fear around the future, that of my families, and my own mortality and well-being. Since the babies had come home, I had developed back pain from constantly bending down to pick them up. I broke the same little toe twice wandering around the bedroom while half asleep. I had also got a stiffness pain in my elbows from holding them and it was all topped off with stress and exhaustion. I had headaches constantly in those months. Thankfully I was only suffering from several bad chest infections and gastritis that could all be treated, and the dark spot was nothing sinister. But It shook me up none the less. At home I was exhausted while trying my best to be of use. I was forty-one-year-old man with four children to raise, a mortgage to pay and food to put on the table. I was off work for almost three weeks and feeling the weight of the responsibility on my shoulders. Financially it hit us hard before Christmas, but It also give me a chance to recover. Being off work also awarded me an opportunity.

Having not had any real paternity leave I got to spend some quality time with the triplets during those weeks the doctors had signed me off work. I also enjoyed the time – despite being so ill - with Frankie and my wife. It became very clear to me that I needed to start taking care of myself physically, as for my emotional wellness I had to stay on top of my meditation practice.

Having triplets is a journey of rolling with the punches. It is a constantly changing situation that you must adapt to or sink. For us it was mostly a case of figuring out the next best move as we went along helped only by Stacey's motherly intuition. Our world became consumed with taking care of the babies. There was no life outside of that bubble in the beginning or for our foreseeable future. I started to understand how my Fathers resentment had set in when my brother was born, followed by myself. He had plans to be a famous musician, his heart set on bigger things until, bang! We turned up, both unplanned, and forced him into a life of struggling parenthood that he was ill-equipped for. We became a burden to him.

The arrival of newborns is all consuming. In all respects. There is little room for self-serving ventures or free time away from the duties at hand, especially in the early days. Every single move we now make revolves around the needs of the triplets. And I cannot afford to resent that. All my past relationships, bar none, failed because of the bitterness and frustration that life seemed to be constantly moving in the opposite direction of my expectations, and of what I felt I deserved (it makes me cringe to think of how I used to be). I also feared responsibility. Partly because I spent most of my time drunk, and partly because I was not great at dealing with life even when sober. My Dad was a young man with dreams to fulfil and problems from childhood bubbling under the surface, and overnight his dreams were squashed by the arrival of my brother. Then thirteen months later I came along and washed the last of them down the drain. And he could never let me, my Mum or my brother forget that because he was unable to forget and forgive himself. And I truly understand his state of mind looking back now. Had I been forced into parenthood whilst still locked in my self-driven existence I would have created only problems to those involved. With the arrival of a child there must be a change in a man's attitude and understanding, not only towards himself, but also towards others and his place in this world. An altruistic spirit must become central to his existence. And the rewards of that selflessness will be endless. It took me a long time to realise this and it was only when I became conscious that I saw it within myself. *I believe the only way a man can really fail at Fatherhood is if he resents his situation, because ultimately it is his children that will pay the price for his bitterness.*

A lot of problems for men arise when their child is seen as the root cause for their failed expectations in life. The wife/partner is different and no longer gives the same sort of attention. You can no longer go out with the boys and get drunk at the weekend without it causing a rift at home. Your golfing handicap takes a hit and you no longer have time to stay for a few in the clubhouse afterwards because Mum's called and needs you to pick up nappies and get back to help with babies. And every time you walk through the door she's wound up, partly because of the stress of looking after demanding babies and partly because you've been out with your mates and haven't been there supporting her.

You have two options when a baby arrives. Sulk and sink into self-pity and create problems for everyone involved. Or go at parenting with the same enthusiasm and zeal you probably put into making a baby in the first place! As controversial as this may sound considering the rise in mental health issues in new Dads, I don't agree with the label of post-natal depression in men. Allow me to explain why before you throw this book in the bin and rain down on me with insults on social media.

What my wife went through emotionally and physically to bring our babies into this world is something I will never go through. I was merely from watching ringside. I get why she didn't want to hear my complaints. My own experience that had me on the brink of depression was not directly caused by the babies. Very important! In my opinion there are ongoing ramifications for the mislabelling of that depression. Telling a man, he is suffering from post-natal

239

depression is heavily suggesting that the baby is somehow directly linked to his suffering. And for a man already feeling the symptoms of suppressed resentment and fear going into fatherhood, directing the focus of those symptoms to the child as the cause, is a terrible mistake. I have worked with many alcoholics and addicts, men who grew to resent their children because of their own failure to deal with the emotional strain of the adjustment. Tragically they see the babies as the number one cause of their own failings, and all their frustration and bitterness winds up directed at them. It happened to my own father. And I was aware of the temptation of walking the same path.

Sleep deprivation and depression go hand in hand. And it's a given that one will suffer with the arrival of newborns. Never, since recovering from my mental health problems, did I ever feel a bigger pull back into depression than I did when sleep deprived. Agitations and fears compounded by tiredness can become overwhelming. If not conscious of the simple cause, we always look for external causes to blame for our internal discomfort, and ego loves to make things complicated. it's always easier to see others as a cause of our issues than to look inward and take responsibility. It's reacting to the negative thinking and self-pity that arises in those periods of stress that cause the real damage, and the resentments that fester as a result. Little grievances become monstrous, the world starts closing in and we are mentally crushed under the pressure. At least it feels that way, when all we really are is tired and lost in our own negative thinking. All new parents will experience this.

Recent studies show that the main causes of depression in new Fathers are...

. Stress and changes to a relationship

. Lack of sleep

. Difficulty adjusting to parenthood

. An unsettled baby

. First time Father

. Difficulty in coping with the change

I don't believe any of the issues listed above are causes. They are simply events, moments in the stream of life beyond our control that bring all sorts of temptation to fear and resent. And the real problem is not the event, although it may seem that way. *The real problem lies in the inability to meet these events without becoming emotionally overwhelmed.* We lose consciousness as the negative emotions and thinking takes hold. To focus on symptoms is a futile exercise. If you have toothache, you can either focus all your attention and time on managing the pain it's creating. Or you can go to the cause and deal with the tooth. And with almost all emotional disturbances -resentment is the number one offender.

It was not the babies that were causing my own struggle to adjust emotionally. It was the improperly met stress around the events that led me into the dark, and through a simple lack of consciousness, I allowed resentment to pierce me. I was defenseless against it. The depression is real, but the cause is dangerously misunderstood. I believe calling it post-natal depression prevents men from owning their real feelings surrounding the birth of their children and accepting the massive changes it makes to their lives. It's not the same thing women get, though it may share some of the same root causes.

I agree whole heartedly there is a real problem among men when it comes to talking about their mental health around the birth of a child, but I also believe that when a man is freed from resentment and shown a way to strengthen from the pressures of new Fatherhood, he can bring a real stability to a home. It's true, as the saying goes - babies don't come with an owner's manual. And many of us were failed by our own fathers who left us rudderless when it comes to dealing with the arrival of our own children. But I believe we are all born with a natural connection to consciousness, a natural discernment allowing us to see right from wrong, an ability to know what to do without struggling for answers no matter what directions our lives took before babies came along, or how well or poorly we were raised.

Our circumstances before babies is irrelevant in the light of the opportunity we have been given as fathers. We can change the course of our children's lives for the better and experience a hugely beneficial change in ourselves. And without experiencing doubt and fear the next right thing to do becomes apparent. You don't need an owner's manual. You already have all you need if you're willing to let go of resentment and see it. That doesn't mean to say the road ahead will be a walk in the park, but hey! If we didn't have the hard times, we'd never have any chances to grow and enjoy the good times.

Chapter 23

Merry Christmas!

I returned to work in better health to finish up before the Christmas break. We had arranged to Stay at Stacey's parents' home for the holidays. It meant more space, extra help and a chance for us to relax a bit. It had been a full year since that last stressful Christmas break, and it was still difficult to fully comprehend all that had happened in that time. I always describe my experience of quitting alcohol for the first time like being spat out of a tornado, staring back at it, and wondering what the hell just happened. It wasn't unlike that feeling as the year ended, except the emotional turmoil I was glancing at had a beautiful purpose for both Stacey and me. It was all worth something.

Stacey spent a full week packing and preparing for our break. On the morning we left, we just about managed to cram into our little seven-seater our luggage, presents and Milo the mini Jack Russel. What we couldn't fit in was loaded into Stacey's nephew's car who was following us up. I realised that morning that I now needed a bigger vehicle, but that would have to wait. The car was enough to get us by until our financial circumstances changed.

It takes around four hours to get to Stacey's parents. We avoided the motorway and travelled on the A-roads which seemed the better option as we would have more opportunities to stop if need be. The babies had never spent so long in a car seat, so we were unsure how it would be for them. Either way we were prepared for a long loud journey. Being fully prepared for anything becomes second nature with triplets, there is no situation my wife and I can't deal with now (except for a norovirus, but that's another horrible story all together). Surprisingly the babies slept and stayed chilled the whole journey. We only needed to stop a couple of times, once to feed and once to change a poopy nappy.

In the car we began talking, not the everyday chit-chat but we talked as we did when we drove to the scans. Occasionally we would both look in the rear-view mirror at our four children sat behind us, then glance at each other both grinning with a sense of pride and achievement. We both agreed it was mad how that year had turned out for all of us. There's no other word for it. My wife having now adjusted to life with the babies had discovered a new strength and confidence within herself. I had watched her emerge into a new woman, no longer fazed by the anxieties that had plagued her leading up to the pregnancy or the depression that crippled her in the months she carried them. I took the chance to tell her how I felt through it all, and how much I had struggled adjusting. She knew I had found it hard, but not the extent I honestly shared with her. She told me that through it all, she never once worried about me, that although I might waver, I would come out the other end. To my wife that's what I do – I endure. She took great strength in the trust she had in me. She explained that if she had the added worry of what I was going through, the babies wouldn't have made it. She was able to focus her attention on them and Frankie.

I was convinced from the start a show of my consistency and love for the triplets, my wife and Frankie would be enough to keep us together, and even though I felt so apart at times and went through some bad days, we had made it. My intuition back then was right. All I had to do was bring emotional stability to our home through patience and tolerance. We had worked together and achieved what seemed impossible at the start.

When I first met my wife, I made it clear from our first conversations over the phone, before we had even laid eyes on each other that I wasn't looking for someone to complete me. I had learned from my many past mistakes, that placing that sort of pressure and reliance on another human being creates an unhealthy attachment. One that always eventually breeds resentment. I had come to realise the futility of resting self-centred expectations on another for no other reason than to fill a need in myself. It's a false idea of love, one that I disastrously bought into as I grew up and wandered into the world. A conscious woman will always see this weakness and run a mile - or grow to resent it. Knowing this, it was clear that If I was to go into any sort of healthy relationship, I would need to stop looking for any sort of approval from others. I walked away from constantly needing reassurance and validation to make me feel whole. And It is how I entered a relationship with Stacey, which is why she doesn't worry about me. It was only when I became lost in fear that I began seeking that validation again. I stepped away from the faith and intuition that guided me through the pregnancy and got needy and controlling, and It brought nothing but tension in those first few months at home with the triplets. Full of fear, my demands were not being met, and I began to resent others for not delivering what I felt I deserved. It was exactly how I used to live before sobriety. Before I woke up.

Drowning in self-pity is no way to be, not if a family is to survive the arrival of babies. Thankfully, I again woke to it in myself before I caused any real damage at home with my relationships. It could easily have all gone horribly wrong for us. The need for me to remain conscious is brought to me every morning when I wake up to a family that rely on me. If I allow myself to get overwhelmed with resentment or fear I will eventually lose them or walk away before I hurt them. I can never let it come to that. Which is why I must remain vigilant to the lower part of myself that feeds on doubt. I will never fully escape the stream of negative thinking 'it' produces, but through daily meditation 'it' shrinks and weakens, and I have learned to observe it without fear. If my babies are to thrive, and my family to stay emotionally healthy, they need to be free to grow in a calm environment. It's my job to stay out of negative emotions and bring a spirit of patience and love to our home. I see this more than ever now, knowing how stress can affect a baby so much in early life.

We reconnected again on that drive, fears subsided, and a clarity shone back in our relationship. We had both found a new mutual respect and love for each other. There was a new trust between us, free of doubt about our future. For the first time in a long time, we found that old comfy place, one a couple newly in love experience. Where everything feels new and exciting. The road ahead was no longer one of uncertainty, it reached out to the horizon, lit with immense purpose. We relaxed enough to talk, laugh and smile the whole journey. We had found each other again and it felt beautiful, if just for that few hours in a break from the madness.

Christmas was an exciting time with a lot to celebrate. We made sure we made a fuss of Frankie, she got a few extra presents from us as a thank you, for all the help she gives with her sisters. We made the most of Di, and everyone one else taking care of the babies. As much as we could, Stacey and I took it easy.

Come boxing day my wife started getting heavily agitated in the early evening. I could see she wasn't right in herself. It was like watching a pressure cooker about to overload. She ended up exploding with insults at her sisters out of her own frustration and stormed up-stairs. She spent the next couple of hours uncontrollably sobbing, saying she didn't know if she had the strength to carry on with it all, that she didn't want to go back to our house and be alone in the day with them anymore.

From the day they were born my wife had knuckled down with the job at hand. She rarely complained. But the breastfeeding and exhaustion had pushed her to the limit, and the stress she was meeting daily wasn't being dealt with consciously - just suppressed and distracted from while focused on the babies. It had gradually built up to boiling point.

When we got to her parents, Stacey had slowed down and when she came to a stop, she hit a hard wall, and with it all the stress, exhaustion, agitation and fear finally caught up with her. It was a release that needed to happen and left her feeling relieved. But it also exposed a need to change the way she dealt with stress going forward. It would be a few months later that she returned to using the meditation exercise. A decision she made that would change everything for her in dealing with our home life. It was after all her arena as a stay at home parent. She now deals with it from a conscious place of patience and tolerance. She doesn't tire so easily. We now truly have a peaceful home.

I really enjoyed that break, I got to take the dog for some good long walks, and made a few phone calls to catch up with friends I hadn't had a normal conversation with for months due to the headspace I had been in. In doing little everyday things that became difficult to do over the last half of that year, I was gradually starting to feel human again. We ate well, slept well, relaxed and enjoyed the holidays. The triplets also took a big step when we started introducing them to real food, just a little at lunchtime to begin with to get them used to a spoon before they got back on the boob. It was nice to be around other people. We had ended up feeling strangely isolated at home, like we lived in a bubble. And unless we went out somewhere, we rarely saw anyone else apart from each other and my Mum when she visited. At least I had my workmates during the day, my wife only had babies to interact with most of the time so for her it was a special trip.

Most of the talk and attention was on the triplets of course. Everyone was still amazed at the events of the year. We were even lucky enough to get a date night in on our anniversary the night before new-year's eve. It was strange going out just the two of us for the first time. But it was a memorable night, not because a great deal happened. But we spent a night at a table in a restaurant, with no worries or concerns, simply free to be ourselves. It was like a first date. We decided to try and make it a regular thing, just to get a break from the relentless routine at home. Date night is now an essential part of our marriage. It was before but now even more-so. They are rare, but when they do happen, we always take the opportunity to talk honestly and reflect on where we are. To see how we are doing as a family and to make sure that we are all moving in the same direction forward. It's a time for meaningful conversation, a personal housecleaning in a way. I love those nights. We saw the New Year in with Stacey's family. I got emotional with the final count-down to midnight. I was filled with gratitude and hope for our future. We had survived a beautiful storm as a family, with healthy children and a stronger marriage. As hard as it had been there was no escaping the miracles that were now entrusted to us. Would I have gone through it all again to have what we have now? Damn right I would.

The drive back was a mixed bag of excitement about going forward, and anticipation in that we were heading back to the grind of daily life. To me it felt like the beginning. The dust had settled from the insane explosion of the previous year and life was now shining with a new perspective. A few nights after settling back in at home we had a new problem. One that began over Christmas and was disrupting any sleep I was getting. Ava had found her voice. She sounded like a mini velociraptor growling and squeaking in her cot. Lacey had also become vocal, mostly babbling and combine that with Blakely's coo's and giggles and all the burping and farting from our musical troupe, our little bedroom came alive in the dark of night.

Stacey for the most managed to sleep unaffected by the sounds of the mini zoo we were now confined in, but I am a light sleeper, and as cute and funny as it was, they were keeping me awake. The other obstacle we had to surmount each night when going to bed was trying to sneak into our bedroom without waking them. We would turn the landing lights off, turn our phones off and tip toe in stealth like. Once in, I had to pass two cots at the end of the bed to get to my side, I would creep around the bed, and suddenly, to my right I would hear the sucking of a thumb in the dark. Followed up by another in the cot next to it. Before we even felt the comfort of our pillow's we were up doing feeds, listening to Mozart for babies and awake for another hour at least before settling them again, except now they just wanted to make noises instead of sleeping. It was time, there was nothing else for it. They had to go...into their own room!

I know of parents who struggled with taking this step. Not

us. When sanity is on the line it doesn't matter how tight the grip on the heartstrings that the bambinos are leaving the bedroom for good, a conscious decision needs to be made. I finished work on the Friday lunchtime and set to finishing the nursery. By two am Saturday morning it was complete. All that was left was to let the paint dry and that night the girls would move into their very own room, one fit for three princesses. That evening we finished the bath and bottle routine around seven pm and tucked them into their growbags, carried them up and placed them into their new beds. We kissed Ava, Lacey and Blakley goodnight and quietly closed the door. We didn't hear a peep out of them that evening, they went straight to sleep and went through twelve hours.

And under our roof, with the storm clouds behind us and the light shining through. life became as normal as it was ever going to be for us.

Chapter 24

Moving forward

Two months after the babies moved into the nursery, I made the decision to begin this book. Ava, Lacey and Blakely were eight months old at the time. The compulsion I felt to put the whole experience down in print was driven by a simple need to document it all and share an honest perspective for others that may find it useful. I believe that anything that might contribute to a family staying the distance through the turbulence of a pregnancy and birth can only be a good thing. Even if you feel that meditation is not for you yet, then at least I hope this book will spark some conversation. People don't always find it easy to admit they are struggling. More-so in the middle of a highly stressful event.

Beginning this book within the first year of life at home with triplets seemed like madness. For a start where would I find the time? But on a conscious level It was something that I had to do. I have never taken on anything like this in my life. With no knowledge or any real idea where to begin with a book I spoke to a couple of friends. Michael, whom I met on my stay in the Orkney islands, and Danny, a man I met after being introduced to the meditation he freely passes on. Both being published and respected authors were able to lend me some valuable tips to make a start. Stephen King was also instrumental in my work. His book 'On writing' became most valuable, a gem for anyone starting out as a serious writer. I was also lucky enough to have touched base with an old friend who I met years ago on an insane trip across Mexico. Who also just happens to be an editor, she has made me work my ass off to get the best out of me as a first-time writer and create something of value in my work, I am forever grateful for her help - even though she fried my brain at times.

The book was written patiently, in each free moment I had an opportunity to sit down and type. In the mornings before work, and prior to the babies waking up was prime time to fire up the laptop and punch out a few more paragraphs. For the most of it though the babies were watching me with great interest tapping away. They were very much involved with the entire process, if only in curiosity.

I probably could have waited for a better time to write it (my wife would probably agree with that statement). But the whole experience was still fresh in my mind and I didn't want to lose any of the colour still bright in the memories. As many other Dads told me, I would forget the first year, and If it became a distant memory It wouldn't be an experience to be able to share with you. It would just be that blurry time in my life that the babies were born.

Much has moved on in the time it has taken to write this book. Life is still challenging with three babies as they continually grow and discover the world around them and the new abilities they find. At this present moment of typing all three are walking. They are behind with their speech which is normal for triplets, they spend so much time communicating with each other that they have little time or reason to talk as we do. They have instead developed their own language and understand each other well. We have absolutely no idea what they may be plotting but they are healthy and content and that is all that matters.

Halfway through writing this book I was diagnosed with a chronic pain disorder originating from my central nervous system. Possibly brought on after getting hit in my car whilst driving home from work one evening. The random nerve pain I began experiencing around my body and face was excruciating at times and made home-life almost impossible to cope with. Stacey was left to deal with me as well as our four daughters as I struggled to adjust to what is a permanent condition. The side-effects of the drugs gave me such a foggy head I wondered at times If I would ever complete this book. So, for the time being I am a stay at home parent, getting under my wife's feet and doing as much as I can to raise my daughters and be of use. Once again it has been the meditation that has become the first point in dealing with a new and challenging situation. After all it is mostly managing the mental side of round the clock pain, the fearful thinking of an uncertain future that pinches me from time to time, depressive and self-pitying thoughts that crop up during a bad flare up that can last for weeks.

If there is anything positive to have come out of it, it is that I have got to share in some of the triplet's big milestones. Amongst their growing bag of new tricks, I got to teach them how to use a spoon and feed themselves breakfast (one less job for us to do). I also got to watch Blakely take her first steps, and what a proud moment that was! Through the up's and downs we have managed to keep the house calm and a strict routine in place, or as calm as possible with three triplet toddlers now charging about the house.

There are times when they all get ill and we are thrown back into sleep deprivation. If only momentarily it serves as a reminder of how hard taking care of three babies can be. I remember well after three nights of them all suffering from ear infections, Stacey and I sat on the sofa exhausted one morning, we just looked at each other and started crying, tears brought on by our dissolving sanity. We were beaten by the emotional strain of dealing with them round the clock. Thankfully it doesn't happen often. But those times are outweighed by the moments we would never have experienced if they were not in our lives. To have all three climbing up on us for a hug is just special. It is that unconditional love and connection we have that makes everything worthwhile. To share in their little moments of triumph when they find a new skill and beam at us with pride.

I could never have imagined in my wildest dreams that becoming a father would bring so much love to our home. And change so much in me on a human and spiritual level. Nothing means more to me than the relationships under my roof. I finally understand the selfless love I was shown back in New Zealand all those years ago and what it means to give without expectation. The importance of my presence and the responsibility that lies in the influence I have in the lives of those who rely on me. The need to continually improve myself is as unavoidable as it is apparent. *If there is one thing I have discovered from my experiences in life, it is that a father's role is just as important as a mother's, and if it isn't treated that way it needs to be.*

To read all this back now Is to revisit an insane year in my life. A snippet of time, with events that have redirected the course of my life and that of my families forever. This book was never intended to be a hard read, in fact I had no intention of sharing some of my life before I met Stacey, but the more I wrote about becoming a parent the more relevant my past became. I hold no resentment towards my past anymore, it has all become something of value in the hard lessons I have learned from those years long gone. Since getting sober I have looked for my dad but to no avail. It would have been good to make amends to him and perhaps be able show him a way to forgive as I discovered. My one hope is that he found his peace somewhere on his journey.

I don't want to put anyone off the experience of having children, or to frighten them about what may be ahead. But it is a very real account of the emotional journey that I and many other Dads of multiples (and singles) go through. Trust me, it gets tough at times. Most important was my discovery of the hope the whole experience brought me. I want others who may be struggling with the pressures of life to see that's it's possible to cope. And more importantly to see that there is a way to be there for those around us when it matters the most, no matter what our past experiences. There is always hope for a better future for our-selves and our children. All it takes is a willingness to change, to wake up and begin to live in the present and face life's pressures from a new perspective. I see more than ever that anything in life is possible with a conscious state of mind. That life doesn't need to be the overwhelming struggle I once found it to be.

Our home has become one of laughter - joy and love. Tough and trying at times, but we have all we need to deal with the inevitable emotional ups and downs ahead. The triplets are content and healthy, thriving in a relatively stress-free environment and it takes work and vigilance from both of us to keep it that way. Life is designed to challenge us, and we have a duty to rise to those challenges, which in turn become the unexpected gifts - opportunities for growth. And as hard and relentless as life can still be at times, the babies continue to shine brightly with a reminder of the life and purpose they have now given us as a family through their arrival. The obstacles they bring us to overcome and learn from will continue - I'm sure. My children and my wife have become my greatest teachers in that respect, the only requirement from me is that I remain willing to learn from each of them, simply by practicing love and patience. I also have plenty of opportunity to learn from the many mistakes I will undoubtedly make as a parent. The trick with failing always lies in not resenting myself when I do get things wrong. To see what I can change in those times of error and to move forward in understanding.

I am excited as to what the future holds for us as we continue to face the inevitable trials of life, the struggles and blessings in turn. But the one thing I'm sure of is that consciously there is nothing my wife and I cannot get through together with a spirit of love central to our home. And as for me, I know I can be the man my family needs me to be. Absent of pride and fear I will be free to raise a healthy family, where kindness and respect for each other is shared. My children will have a start in life that will hopefully set them up positively as they grow in their formative years, they will not begin their lives with the same emotional pressures as I did. That cycle of fear and resentment that ran through the generations of men before me - has stopped with me. As their father I will show them how to practice the principles of love and tolerance, so they may face life with courage in all they do. The very same principles that contributed to their safe arrival, and now their calm home environment.

As I write this Stacey and Frankie are out, taking a break and enjoying a pampering day. Ava is pawing at my leg for a cuddle. Lacey has her leg stuck under the sofa and is about to start crying any second and Blakely is sitting on the floor playing happily with her toys, babbling at the world. So, I have things to be getting on with. And as for life now, I wouldn't change a single thing. And I thank God with everything in me for every exhausting, farty, dribble filled minute of it.

The meditation

Firstly, this isn't a sales pitch. You are either at a point in your life where you are ready to begin meditating - or are not. Only you will know this. This is not to be approached lightly in the sense that it is a very powerful awakening exercise. One that will change the way you view the world and your relationship with it. Especially in your relationships with others.

It is a way to build resilience to stress through a very special conscious awareness. It can be uncomfortable to begin with as you awaken, separating from the noisy stream of thought. It is a unique way to observe the chatter of the overactive mind and remain unaffected by it, leaving you free to live in the present moment - free from resentment and fear. To live consciously as we were all born to do.

Throughout these pages I have referred to this simple meditation practice a lot, and for good reason. It has changed the course of my life like nothing else I've ever encountered. It has brought emotional stability into my home-life and changed the way I carry myself in the world and treat those around me, simply by being still and becoming conscious daily.

My wife also practices the same exercise after returning to it in the first year of the triplets arriving. For Stacey, it has changed the way she deals with life as a full time Mum. Neither of us struggle with stress as a result. It has given us the basis for a loving home.

I have also had the pleasure of seeing others commit to a life of conscious awareness and they too, are dealing with life successfully. Free from the debilitating effects of stress and the obsessive thinking and behaviours that can manifest as a result.

If you feel you may benefit from this free exercise (there is nothing to buy or learn, it's completely free) follow this link to a friend of mine's website. Danny Schwarzhoff Snr has dedicated his life to helping others through Non-contemplative meditation. Believe me, It's a game changer.

This is the link.

https://schwarzhoffmedia.com/non-contemplative-meditation/

Useful sites

www.Tripletdad.blog – my personal blog, where I share regular posts on homelife and dealing with the inevitable ups and downs of fatherhood.

Better men – Better fathers – A closed Facebook group. A community of men dedicated to improvement. Also, a place to find solutions with problems like drug and alcohol addiction.

Multiple dad's sanctuary – A closed Facebook group dedicated to helping all dads of multiples through shared support and experience become better fathers along their journey. An Australian site with a worldwide membership.

Dads of Triplets - American based site on Facebook exclusively for dads of triplets. With members from all over the world ready to offer support and experience.

Dads of twins and multiples (worldwide) – A Facebook

page of shared experience and a wealth of information from dads on the multiple journey.

UK Triplet and quad mummies – A closed Facebook group for expectant mums and those already with children. (My wife assures me that with a quick search there are many multiple groups for Mums on fb)

Tamba.org.uk - Twins and multiples birth association - A charity run organisation focused on educating and supporting parents of multiples. On the website you will find helpful information on all things multiple. If you join, membership also includes discount at many high street outlets.

A meditative parent

Printed in Poland
by Amazon Fulfillment
Poland Sp. z o.o., Wrocław